"This book is a must-read for anyone navigating life's transitions. *Hinge Moments* teaches us how to honor God through the chaos of change, embrace life's decision moments, and come out stronger on the other side."

**Kay C. James,** president of Heritage Foundation

"We live in a world where the only constant seems to be change. Michael Lindsay identifies key factors that will help you navigate transition points in your life, personally and professionally. It will help you not only survive but thrive the sea of uncertainty."

**Mark Batterson,** author of *The Circle Maker* and lead pastor of National Community Church

"The changes we face in life are always unique and personal, but Michael Lindsay brings comfort and confidence in the understanding that these individual experiences also reflect the universal human condition. A delightful treasury of stories, science, and wisdom, *Hinge Moments* will enlighten and encourage you in whatever momentous transition might come your way."

**Karen Swallow Prior,** author of *On Reading Well: Finding the Good Life Through Great Books*

"If there is a time for everything, as the Bible says, then there is a time for gifted leaders to move from one season of life or place of service to the next. This beautifully written book is a handbook for life's transitions—from the restlessness that often precedes a change of calling all the way through to a new season of meaningful, productive leadership. Michael Lindsay is the perfect guide. Through his extensive research and influential work in higher education, Dr. Lindsay knows more about leadership than just about anyone. In this inspiring book he uses stories from his extensive network of fellow leaders—as well as history and the Bible—to help his readers get and stay prepared for whatever comes next."

**Philip Ryken,** president of Wheaton College

"Succinct yet profound, Lindsay's accessible storytelling offers comfort that you can become a master of adaptation by continuing to trust in the Lord's reliable plan for your many vocations."

**Ben Sasse,** US senator from Nebraska, former president of Midland University

"Whether unexpected or carefully planned, transitions in life are inevitable. In *Hinge Moments*, Michael Lindsay delivers brilliant insights drawn from his deep faith and years of leadership to help us make these pivotal times in our own lives into opportunities for growth and enlightenment."

**Arthur C. Brooks,** author and professor, Harvard Kennedy School and Harvard Business School

# HINGE

## MOMENTS

### D. MICHAEL LINDSAY

WITH DAVIS METZGER

## MAKING
## THE MOST
## OF LIFE'S
## TRANSITIONS

ivp

An imprint of InterVarsity Press
Downers Grove, Illinois

InterVarsity Press
P.O. Box 1400, Downers Grove, IL 60515-1426
ivpress.com
email@ivpress.com

InterVarsity Press® is the book-publishing division of InterVarsity Christian Fellowship/USA®, a
movement of students and faculty active on campus at hundreds of universities, colleges, and schools
of nursing in the United States of America, and a member movement of the International Fellowship of
Evangelical Students. For information about local and regional activities, visit intervarsity.org.

All Scripture quotations, unless otherwise indicated, are taken from The Holy Bible, New International
Version®, NIV®. Copyright © 1973, 1978, 1984, 2011 by Biblica, Inc.™ Used by permission of Zondervan.
All rights reserved worldwide. www.zondervan.com. The "NIV" and "New International Version" are
trademarks registered in the United States Patent and Trademark Office by Biblica, Inc.™

While any stories in this book are true, some names and identifying information may have been
changed to protect the privacy of individuals.

The publisher cannot verify the accuracy or functionality of website URLs used in this book beyond the
date of publication.

Cover design and image composite: David Fassett
Interior design: Jeanna Wiggins
Image: abstract sunburst: © -1001- / iStock / Getty Images Plus

ISBN 978-0-8308-4179-0 (print)
ISBN 978-0-8308-4180-6 (digital)

Printed in the United States of America ♾

InterVarsity Press is committed to ecological stewardship and to the conservation of natural resources
in all our operations. This book was printed using sustainably sourced paper.

**Library of Congress Cataloging-in-Publication Data**
A catalog record for this book is available from the Library of Congress.

P   25   24   23   22   21   20   19   18   17   16   15   14   13   12   11   10   9   8   7   6   5   4   3   2   1

Y   42   41   40   39   38   37   36   35   34   33   32   31   30   29   28   27   26   25   24   23   22   21

## DEDICATED TO

Davis, Herman, Kurt, Rebecca, and William,

*wonderful partners for navigating*

*life's hinge moments*

# CONTENTS

# INTRODUCTION

IN A QUIET HOSPITAL ROOM in North Carolina, an eager young doctor with a bright future evaluates his elderly patient with not much future left at all. She has a terminal heart condition, inoperable. All he can do is treat her symptoms and pain as the two of them wait for her time to run out.

As the physician visits the dying woman during his daily rounds, they gradually get to know one another. During one particularly poignant conversation, he learns that the woman is a deeply religious Christian. As a confident atheist, he assumes that as her condition deteriorates, her faith will do the same, as she realizes her God is not coming to the rescue. Yet with every passing day, his patient's faith seems to grow stronger even as her body weakens.

Having been exposed years earlier to the writings of Heisenberg, Dirac, and Einstein, the doctor finds his patient's religious beliefs antiquated but charming. But then, he is taken aback by her forthright inquiry: "Doctor, I have been telling you what I believe, but what do *you* believe?"

It's not that he takes no joy in what his patient would call "creation." Rather, he finds the universe deeply satisfying. He has long relished the idea that it can be understood and explained in discrete mathematical formulae—that it can present no dilemma that a robust theorem cannot answer. But in this case, he is shaken a bit when asked about *belief*. He murmurs something about the beauty of the natural world and leaves the conversation with a degree of unease.

He is one of the best trained scientists of his generation. By his own reckoning, there is no one who better understands the systems and laws that keep nature running. But he is deeply unsettled by the way the dying woman sleeps peacefully in her hospital bed while he lies awake each night haunted by her question. How can she be so confident of her view of the world and her place in it? Shouldn't she, at death's doorstep, be the sleepless one?

He becomes convinced that his inability to answer her question or find consolation in his view of the mechanical universe is intellectually unacceptable. In search of a fresh perspective, he visits a local minister, who hands him a book by Oxford don C. S. Lewis, which he reads cover to cover. Over the next two years, the young physician reads voraciously about Buddhism, Christianity, Hinduism, Islam, and Judaism, examining the data about their roots and their claims, seeking to find one that would help him satisfactorily answer the dying woman's question.

Ultimately, while hiking in Oregon's Cascade Mountains, he comes to the conclusion that the claims of Christianity best explain what he sees around him. He begins to embrace the faith of his former patient, who had begun a kind of "cascade" within him with her one honest question. His radical internal shift doesn't change much on the outside. He still loves his work as a scientist and doesn't intend to redirect his efforts into religious service. His sense of meaning and purpose, however, has refocused entirely. Indeed, this faith decision would become the fulcrum for a career that would eventually reach the apex of scientific renown and public service.

This is the story of Francis Collins, one of our generation's leading scientific authorities. Not only did he go on from that North Carolina residency program to lead the five research teams that mapped the human genome—the most significant scientific discovery of our lifetime—but he also held one of the longest directorships in history of the National Institutes of Health, appointed to the role first by President Obama and then reappointed by President Trump. His faith decision became a significant turning point, one that not only shaped his life but— by virtue of his leadership roles in the decades since—the lives of many others.

## WHAT ARE HINGE MOMENTS?

There are particular moments in our own lives that are very much like Collins's awkward instant when he had no answer to his patient's inquiry. We realize, sometimes in a flash, that something has to change—is going to change—whether we like it or not. Collins could never go back to his spiritual complacency. He had to move in one direction or another.

What follows these instances will depend intrinsically on the decisions we make and the actions we take. These are *hinge moments*—opportunities to open (or to close) doors to various pathways of our lives.

Such moments are axial by nature, representing a fixed time, place, or event with consequences for the rest of our days. Getting them right can change our lives for the better. Getting them wrong can pose problems for years to come. Each of us is given a finite number of these hinge moments in life. In total, they may represent only a few hundred minutes out of our total lives of seventy or eighty years, but they have an outsized impact on the other thirty-seven million minutes of our time on earth. For Francis Collins, arriving at a better answer for what he believed about the nature of the universe and the afterlife began when he opened the door to exploring the possibility of universal truth. And by his own account, his life was forever changed.

But there were actually two hinge moments in the hospital room that day. Even as Dr. Collins was encountering a pivotal instance early in his career, that woman in the hospital bed was approaching one of her last. After all, how we approach death—for ourselves and those we love—is itself a decision.

Some periods of transition are predictable in their arrival. You plan to ask a certain someone to marry you, and you plan for months—even years—in advance. Or you start contemplating your college decision as a junior in high school. Or you start planning for the birth of your first child the moment you see a positive pregnancy test. These are the sorts of significant transitions that we can anticipate, even prepare for. Death is the last of these hinge moments we face in life. The hospitalized woman knew hers was coming, and she slept soundly because she felt prepared for it.

But some profound changes arrive in the blink of an eye. A beloved family member is killed in an accident, or your boss tells you that your job is being eliminated. And because these kinds of bombshell transitions entail uncharted territory, we cannot always lean on the typical securities of our environment. Francis

Collins could not have anticipated the hinge moment that was barreling his way that fateful night. Usually, neither can we.

## NAVIGATING SEASONS OF CHANGE

By the time they have turned eighteen, most Americans will have moved at least twice. Most thirty-year-olds will have moved six times. By the end of our lives, most of us will have pushed that number up to eleven.[1] This highly mobile way of life is mirrored in our career habits as well. The average American worker holds ten different jobs before the age of forty,[2] and this job transience is only expected to increase in the years ahead.[3] Add to these the slew of major life changes such as college or vocational training, marriage, and having children, and it becomes clear how many different phases our lives actually have. For all of us there is only one thing that remains the same—the fact that nothing does.

All these major decisions, though different in nature, are the same in that they determine our future trajectory. There are no neutral choices here—no loitering on the threshold of destiny. Each of these moments will either help or hurt us, depending on how we handle the transition between one space and the next. And we're talking about when things are *normal*.

The coronavirus pandemic of 2019 and 2020 turned the lives of millions of people around the world upside down. At one point, the unemployment rate in the US neared 15 percent. That is higher than the peak unemployment of the Great Recession, and the largest recorded unemployment in American history since the Great Depression. Couple this with the fact that there are tens of millions more who are wondering if COVID-19 will lay waste to their own careers, and it becomes clear that this crisis could produce more hinge moments than this country has seen in generations. It is difficult to overstate just how much is changing. Companies are rethinking how they do business. Workers are looking for new places and ways to work. Families are postponing having children.[4] Universities are rapidly coming to terms with what it means to be an institution with no students on campus. As a result of all of this, tens of millions of people in this country are undergoing major transitions, both voluntary and otherwise.

Most of the things that happen over the course of our lives can be readily characterized as "good" or "bad." Winning an award, getting married, or enrolling in your dream school: good. Losing a loved one or getting the virus: bad. Periods of transition are different; even the best and most welcome transitions are still the results of *change*, and that is universally unsettling. This is what sets transitions apart from the other barriers and blessings in life. Typically, when the good and the bad come knocking at our door, we have roots and community to laugh or cry with us. The problem with hinge moments is that they have to be managed in the disorienting space between communities, in the time between the uprooting of the old and the planting of the new.

## HOW TRANSITIONS SHAPE US

Nearly a decade ago, I moved from what I thought was my dream job teaching sociology at Rice University in Texas to become the president of Gordon, a Christian liberal arts college on Boston's North Shore. It was initially not a move I was looking to make. My family and I were very happy in Houston.

It all began when I answered the phone one morning and was asked if I might be interested in applying to become Gordon's next president. I thought it might be an honor to serve as a college president someday, "But not now," I told the recruiter. "Maybe in ten to fifteen years."

Several weeks following that phone call, our family encountered an unexpected hinge moment. One rainy morning in early November, my thirty-two-year-old cousin was driving to work when he saw the car of a highway patrol officer hydroplane off the wet pavement. My cousin pulled over to make sure the driver was okay. As he approached the patrol car, a tractor-trailer driver behind him slammed on his brakes, causing the rig to jackknife, swing around, and strike my cousin, killing him instantly. I still cannot believe he is gone. He left behind a wife and three young children.

In the days that followed, I came to realize that we are not promised tomorrow, that my plans for what I might do in ten to fifteen years might not always be possible. I woke up to the fact that doors don't stay open forever. The next week, I called the recruiter and asked if they were still accepting applications.

In truth, I never thought I would be selected. But I had been studying leadership for many years, and now I wondered what it might be like to step into such a meaningful leadership role myself. I ended up being selected for the Gordon presidency. Looking back, I can see exactly how the change that would move our family from Texas to Massachusetts all began in that hinge moment on that rainy November morning. The challenge with life is that we have to live it moving forward, but we really only understand it looking back. Every day offers the promise of preparing us to best respond to the next hinge moment of our lives.

## THE PLATINUM LEADERS AND
## THEIR TRANSITIONS

That move turned out to be one of the best decisions of my life, but it certainly had some lessons to teach me. I have come to understand that to study leadership is to study the science of transitions. I dedicated ten years of my life to conducting the PLATINUM study,[5] the largest empirical study of American leaders in history. I conducted full-length interviews, and my team and I performed analyses on 550 of America's top figures, including presidents Carter and Bush alongside leaders of hundreds of Fortune 500 firms and their nonprofit equivalents. It was through this project that I came to interview Francis Collins and learn his story. The core leadership findings from that study are detailed in my previous work, *A View from the Top*. The most extraordinary leaders—those I called "platinum leaders"—were the ones who demonstrated remarkable resilience and resourcefulness.

As helpful as that book has been, however, it overlooks an important topic: how to handle well the hinge moments life presents us, whether we planned for them or not. As I have reflected on the research and interviews in recent years, it has become clear to me that like each of us, those platinum-level leaders had numerous opportunities for transition and change in their lives. Sometimes it was something they made happen themselves. Sometimes the changes were forced on them. Sometimes it was being fired, or the death of a loved one. Other times it was a sense of restlessness that called them to some new thing. For these platinum leaders, moments of change were almost always converted into moments of opportunity that propelled them upward. I am convinced that what made the difference in their lives was how they managed times of change, how they responded to their hinge moments.

## HOW HINGE MOMENTS DEFINE US

As a Black girl born to an unwed teenager in rural Mississippi during the 1950s, her prospects in life were challenging, to say the least. She lived with her grandmother for a number of years and was so poor that she would wear potato sacks as dresses to school. Her relatives passed her around from town to town as they were willing, with several of them sexually abusing her along the way. Eventually she went to live permanently with her biological father and found some measure of stability: he prioritized her education and bolstered her self-esteem. Her life improved. Her high school peers voted her most popular, and she won Miss Black Tennessee at age seventeen. With that accomplishment, she landed a talk-radio job as a rising star. In a few years' time, WJZ Television in Baltimore had hired her as one of the youngest (and only Black female) news anchors in the country.

Oprah Winfrey's unlikely rise from poverty to the six o'clock news is a testament to her charisma and talent in front of the camera. But just when it seemed everything was going great, she was fired. The producers criticized her as dull and claimed that she frequently mispronounced words on air. She had never expected this kind of life change, and by her own account, it was a crushing blow. As she put it, "I was devastated, devastated!"[6] Her life, which had finally achieved a degree of success, was teetering on the verge of collapse back into the cycle of heartache and suffering that she had escaped as a young woman. Since high school she had dreamt of a news job; everything she had worked for was now over—and with abrupt certainty.

As some consolation for the firing, the news producer offered her a spot on a failing talk show called *People Are Talking*. No one really believed that she or the show would survive long, so it was an easy way for the producers to move her on. Facing no alternative, Oprah took the job. Gradually, her on-air personality blossomed. She had opportunities to demonstrate empathy and care, two attributes of her personality that she once resisted in her quest to become an impartial news anchor. Over time her show became extremely popular, and she eventually resettled and created *The Oprah Winfrey Show*, which premiered nationally in 1986. Within a few years, Winfrey's show had beaten out Phil Donahue's as the number-one daytime talk show. The next thirty years included countless honors and accolades, consistently shattering ceilings for women and racial minorities. In 2018 she was named one of the five hundred richest people on earth and was the first Black woman to win the Cecil B. DeMille Award for lifetime achievement at the Golden Globes.

Oprah's is a story about a life transition that no one, including Winfrey herself, could have predicted. Her meteoric rise has opened doors for millions of other women and people of color. But by her own telling, the career setback in Baltimore was the catalyst for a change that made all her subsequent success possible. When you are handed that pink slip by your boss and shown the door, it will not seem like you are bouncing upward. But if you are prepared when these critical moments occur, you—like Winfrey—can transform a normal transition (even an unwelcome one) into a stellar hinge moment.

Not every moment is a defining moment, but some transitions have a disproportionate impact on our happiness, our contribution to society, and our family's well-being. It behooves us to prepare for them very carefully, learning from those who have already demonstrated mastery in this area. This book contains not only stories and lessons of success and faithfulness from those kinds of leaders but stories of failure as well. Sometimes, in God's providence, people were able to recover from early mistakes and return stronger than ever. Other times, a single transition executed poorly solidified the high-water mark for their career. In either case, by learning from the experiences of others, we can manage our own life changes more effectively than if we tried to figure it all out ourselves. In uncertain and tumultuous times, taking hold of every advantage we can is essential. There is no better advantage than wisdom gained early, and the college years often provide helpful preparation.

Prashan De Visser left his native land of Sri Lanka in the midst of a civil war, which raged for many years between two of the country's largest ethnic groups. He, like countless others, came to believe that those in the other group were the source of the nation's troubles and that if they would just go away, everything would be better. But he aspired to attend university in the United States, and he came to Gordon College.

At Gordon, De Visser thrived, studying international affairs and eventually becoming student body president. Under the mentorship of Gordon faculty and staff, he began to read widely and engage Christian thinkers from many different perspectives on peacemaking, reconciliation, global conflict, and human nature. For his undergraduate thesis, De Visser studied models of peacebuilding in South Africa and Northern Ireland. This began a change process in his life that eventually compelled him to found an organization called Sri Lanka Unites, which has now grown to an international movement in over a dozen countries and on four continents. It's a youth organization focused on grassroots reconciliation that has garnered international recognition. He learned that 70 percent of young people in Sri Lanka had no friends outside their own ethnic group, and his organization is now working to bridge these divides. Queen Elizabeth II recognized him as a Commonwealth Point of Light when he was just thirty-three years old.

But when De Visser boarded the plane for Boston, he had no idea that he was embarking on a journey that would end up changing not only his life but the lives of thousands of others. As is the case for most of us, he simply took the next logical step in his journey. But that step eventually led him to entirely new places. Also, his life bears witness to the reality that transitions (even permanent-feeling ones) may not last forever. You may be called out of one place or season in your life for a time just to be sent back into the fray. Transitions that take us away from things may simply be stops along the way back home.

## STAGES OF TRANSITION

Each of us experiences transition through a series of stages, similar to the stages of grief we experience during seasons of loss or pain. There is a temporal aspect to these stages since we process them over time and in a particular order, but they can go fast or slow depending on the circumstances. And the phases bring on differing degrees of confidence as we move through them.

We begin a given transition with a stable measure of assurance because we start in a relatively settled environment, complete with sources of support and recognized routines. But then as we enter a stage of discernment about a possible change, our confidence wanes. We feel a mix of anxiety and hope, of nervous excitement about possibilities but also some degree of dread about the changes that may be required. We eventually reach our lowest point of confidence at the liminal moment in between our old and new ways of life.

At this intersection we know the least about our future but also recognize that our past will no longer provide the same degree of support for what lies ahead. This state of being betwixt and between can be debilitating, but we can also marshal creative energy at this unique spot. Gradually, the tide turns, and we move into a new space. In this landing phase, we meet many new people and encounter new opportunities. Every interaction provides an additional data point that allows us to gain our bearings and begin settling in. This, in turn, leads to a phase of integration. We begin to trust others, and they come to find us trustworthy; in so doing, we develop deeper ties that supplant some of the previous relational networks we needed to thrive.

Gradually, we emerge with a stronger degree of confidence and confirmation than when we began the whole process. The full range of experiences brought on by this change—the good and the bad, the opportunities and the challenges—become sources of strength for our forward journey. This, in turn, allows us (through godly reflection) to make sense of it all and to develop a fuller sense of inspiration for our lives. In turn, we become a resource for others who are in earlier phases of their own transitions. Finally, we reach a stage of realization in which we recognize that the whole experience has allowed us to mature and deepen in ways that would have been impossible without the change.

In God's providence, this is the typical way we experience the internal process of transition that accompanies external change. This book will walk through these seven stages of transition, relating stories of those who have navigated the phases successfully and offering suggestions of how you can make the most of each stage God brings you through.

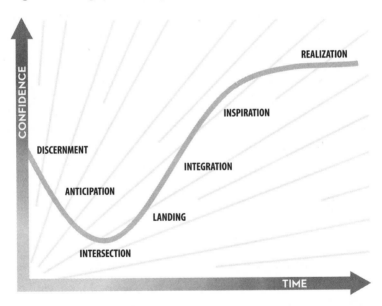

## FAILURE IS THE WAKE-UP CALL TO TRANSITION

External forces like the death of a loved one, an uncomfortable encounter with a dying patient, or the various effects of COVID-19 may force changes in our lives that we did not initiate. If you are laid off at work because of downsizing, that is not your fault.

However, if you are fired from work for poor job performance, that is on you. Though seemingly different, both scenarios force you into a season of change. They are both moments that demand attention and provide opportunities for success or failure. I found that most successful transitions made by platinum leaders were preceded by some initial concerns, mistakes, or unintended missteps. The most perceptive people I studied were able to notice patterns and strategically prepare for what they sensed would be some sort of change to their lives. They knew that their responsibility was not to accurately predict the future but rather to pay attention and to learn and grow. They gained these insights through prayer and reflection, by seeking godly counsel, and by staying connected to the Lord as they sought to learn and grow.

One of the most valuable takeaways from the PLATINUM study is that the most successful people in our society are not altogether different from you or me. A number of them came from humble backgrounds and experienced the basic life chances most of us are given. There are many reasons the top leaders of today got where they are, but a common thread is their excellent management of the transitional events in their lives. For many of them, faith in Jesus Christ sustained them in the difficult moments and stretched them to become better people. They developed habits and spiritual practices that supported them when hard times came. Every one of us has a number of these hinge moments in life where our trajectory can be altered. If we mismanage them, we increase the odds of ending up on a chute rather than a ladder. But the world is filled with people who, through God's guiding hand and divine wisdom, are able to see these moments as chances to learn and grow—leveraging twists and turns into new opportunities.

# 1

# APPROACHING THE DOORS IN OUR LIVES

## CONSIDERING A CHANGE

*For everything there is a season,*
*and a time for every matter under heaven:*

*a time to be born, and a time to die;*
*a time to plant, and a time to pluck up what is planted;*
*a time to kill, and a time to heal;*
*a time to break down, and a time to build up.*

ECCLESIASTES 3:1-3 (ESV)

I WAS SIX YEARS OLD WHEN the floods destroyed my home. We had not been planning on moving, but it is hard to argue with five feet of water. The Pearl River runs from central Mississippi down to the Gulf of Mexico, passing straight through my hometown of Jackson. The rains that caused the flood had fallen upstream of us, out of our sight. Such is often the case with sudden changes: their causes are unseen and often entirely unrelated to us. The comptroller general of the United States eventually determined that the flooding had been so severe because efforts to fight and mitigate it were "hampered by a lack of coordination among federal, state, and local agencies."[1] It was not my family's fault that the rains were three times heavier than normal that spring, or that the Army Corps of Engineers had not communicated with the local authorities. It was not our fault that the flood waters rose higher than estimates predicted and poured into our home. Even though none of this was our fault, one terrible evening it became our problem.

Change is like a flood. It often comes on quickly, and you might not see it coming. But transition is different. Transition is a gradual process that follows a major change in life. If you quit your job and move to a new city to start a new job, that change happens quickly. One day you are working for one company; the next day you are working for another. Or for younger people, one day you are living at home with your parents; the next day you are living at college. These changes are instantaneous and definite. You can circle the day of the big move on your calendar. But it is harder to pinpoint precisely when you will have fully transitioned into the new place. Thankfully, unlike change, most transitions are anticipatable, and we have some measure of control over how they play out.

I became the president of Gordon College by a vote of the board of trustees on March 26, 2011. But if you asked me when it was that I fully transitioned to *being* the president of the school, I could not tell you. I never woke up one day and thought, "Ah yes, today is the day I finally feel at ease in my new job." But I did eventually enter that state. This is because unlike changes, which are instantaneous and definite, transitions are gradual and imprecise. They are a process, not a moment.

At their core, transitions are the internal adjustments by which we reorient ourselves to new environments, new experiences, and new seasons of life. These changes wear different guises at different stages in our lives, but for many of us the first major change we experience is our graduation from high school. The transition to college life or the job market comes more gradually. No college student feels at home on the first day of classes. But mastering this transition—weaning ourselves from familiar places and habits and embracing independence from our childhood lives—sets us up for future success.

Changes disrupt our lives and move us into new seasons, where we must begin the process of transition. Sociologist Ann Swidler has written persuasively about the difference between "settled" and "unsettled" times. Settled times consist of "traditions and common sense; [within which we] refine and reinforce skills, habits, and modes of experience."[2] These settled times are where most of us spend nearly our entire lives. They are the familiar and comfortable seasons of life in which our environments and habits are well understood. We are guided within them by routine because that is how we simplify and make sense of life. In the *un*settled times, not routines but new ideas are the forces driving us forward. In these times, we "create new strategies for action." These unsettled times are what I usually call transitionary periods.

Our lives are an ongoing movement between settled and unsettled spaces. We use familiarity and routine for as long as we can,

> At their core, transitions are the internal adjustments by which we reorient ourselves to new environments, new experiences, and new seasons of life.

but when change occurs, we are often forced through new doorways and have to adapt to new ways of thinking, new modes of acting. Change moves us out of our previous settled time; transition moves us into the next one. While changes are significant to our lives, it is the success of our transitions that will determine our satisfaction and effectiveness in the days and years to come—whether we will succeed in college or find satisfaction in our new job. This chapter is about discerning how to respond to the unsettling moments when change is around the corner, whether we chose it or not. How well we handle these moments makes a world of difference.

## BE PREPARED

There are at least three kinds of changes we face: those we wouldn't choose but we can see coming, those we choose ourselves, and those that flood our homes at two in the morning. The first two offer us some choice about how and when we pack our bags; the third offers us none.

I interviewed Jamie Dimon, current CEO of JPMorgan Chase (the largest bank in the United States) and previous cofounder of the financial services conglomerate Citigroup (the third largest). While at Citigroup, he experienced a sudden, involuntary change. At the time, he was serving as president, the company was growing, and by all accounts, his employees and board were pleased with his work. Yet one Sunday afternoon, a senior executive

> There are at least three kinds of changes we face: those we wouldn't choose but we can see coming, those we choose ourselves, and those that flood our homes at two in the morning.

reached out for a quick chat—and ended up firing Dimon. He was forced out over a weekend. That evening, as he told his family what had happened, his youngest daughter asked if they would have to move out of their house and live in the streets. Jamie Dimon was certainly not penniless, so his daughter was not going to sleep in the streets. But his story illustrates an important point. It does not matter how successful, wealthy, or good you are at your job: a major life change is never more than a phone call away.

Because of their unpredictability, unexpected changes are often the most difficult to handle. But just because something is unpredictable does not mean it is unpreparable. In fact, the unpredictability of these changes actually makes the scope of preparation quite narrow. The best way to prepare for an unseen transition is to keep in mind how close one could be and to develop the virtues—such as humility, courage, and self-control—we will need to make good choices when the hinge moment presents itself.

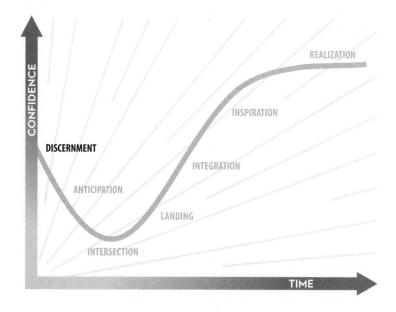

In the phase of discernment, we benefit from practices that help still the soul. Silence and solitude, meditation and self-examination are some of the best ways to manage the mix of emotions we feel during this phase of our transition. God speaks most often not through a megaphone or a billboard but through a still, small voice. The clearest way to hear God is to become quiet enough to be attentive. As Isaiah 30:21 reminds us, "Whether you turn to the right or to the left, your ears will hear a voice behind you, saying, 'This is the way; walk in it.'" But God primarily speaks from behind—not in front of—us. That means we usually have to take the first step even when we are unsure of the way forward. And, of course, not every opportunity is one we should pursue. Sometimes moving is not the best move. But before we can reach that conclusion, we have to actively seek the Lord's guidance and listen for God's leading in our lives.

When properly understood, the inevitability of future transitions is not a cause for fear but a reason for gratitude for what is and preparation for what will be. We can trust in God's goodness because we serve a Lord who is familiar with the troubles of this world but who has also overcome them. There are simple things you can do to prepare for the unexpected, such as keeping your résumé up to date or getting a new appraisal for your home. But these preparations will not remove the suffering from a future transition. Such pain does not come from the small tasks we have to complete when we move but rather from the sudden removal of the structures that support us in the settled times of life. Therefore, being mentally and spiritually prepared for changes you cannot anticipate is the best way to take the teeth out of a transition. Spiritual disciplines—such as keeping a daily gratitude journal or memorizing Scripture—are resources we can draw upon in times of upheaval and uncertainty. Indeed, daily practices that improve our character are the most straightforward way to prepare for the unexpected.

## RESPECT YOUR RESTLESSNESS

For those who are made particularly uncomfortable by unforeseen change, there is good and bad news. The good news is that sometimes we get to pick the timing of our transitions; the bad news is that sometimes we get to pick the timing of our transitions. Voluntary transitions may lack the sting of unforeseen change, but they bring distinct challenges of their own. Almost always, these voluntary transitions in the lives of my PLATINUM study subjects began with a feeling of restlessness or dissatisfaction. It seems that sometimes if we stay in the "settled times" for too long, we grow tired of the routine and the comfort, and begin to crave something new. A feeling of restlessness is not cause enough to quit your day job, but you should listen to it.

> When properly understood, the inevitability of future transitions is not a cause for fear but a reason for gratitude for what is and preparation for what will be.

I got to know Bruce Kennedy a year before he died. Bruce had served as the most successful CEO in the history of Alaska Airlines. In less than ten years on the job, he matured the company from an obscure, regional carrier to the nationwide brand it is today, growing its revenue tenfold. And then, all of a sudden, he stepped away:

> I started getting restless in about my tenth year . . . and I couldn't quite put my finger on it. . . . Somehow it wasn't

holding the fascination for me that it had. I was on the board
of Mission Aviation Fellowship . . . and after the board
meeting, we decided to drive over to Palm Springs and just
go into a motel [to] read the Bible and pray, for guidance specifically on this issue. . . . I had just a very clear . . . understanding at that time that my time of stewardship with
Alaska was coming to an end, and that I was to pass it on,
step down. I was weeping, I was just openly sobbing.

Bruce was one of the first people I interviewed, and the story of
his deeply emotional response to an oncoming transition struck
me. As I interviewed others, I realized that his story was not
unique. Time and time again, I saw people who, at the top of their
careers, suddenly walked away. For some, it was a way to resolve
tensions over work-life balance. For many others, it was a matter
of needing a chance to self-renew after many years of long, hard
work. A sudden break afforded a chance to undertake something
entirely different. And for a few, it was a response to a sense of
calling they had been feeling for a while and finally decided to act.

Bruce's story sheds light on how we might approach these voluntary transitions. First, a transition is not always an escape from
a bad time or tragic event. Many times transitions come even as
the days are good, long, and sunny. But for everything there is a
season, and oftentimes a sense of restlessness is the first sign that
it is time to move along.

The second lesson from Bruce's story is that he didn't keep
his thoughts and deliberations to himself. Rather, he did the
two things I found most common among successful people as
they were facing a hard life decision. First, he sought counsel.
The advice of a trusted confidant is invaluable at the onset of a

transition. For Bruce it was his wife, a very natural choice. But it could also be a mentor, a pastor, a coach—anyone who can serve as a sounding board. Having long-term mentors and trusted friends is essential during these seasons.

There is also another source of counsel and wisdom: faith in Christ. In transition, people of faith know not only that God has ordered their steps but also that he is responsive to petition and prayer. That's why in addition to consulting others, Bruce also prayed for guidance and confirmation. For many, Paul's words to the Philippians are especially comforting in seasons of change: "Do not be anxious about anything, but in everything by prayer and supplication with thanksgiving let your requests be made known to God. And the peace of God, which surpasses all understanding, will guard your hearts and your minds in Christ Jesus" (Philippians 4:6-7 ESV).

Finally, and most soberingly, Bruce reminds us that leaving is tough. It often really hurts. But leaving a settled time opens the doorway to new possibilities, to even more enriching experiences. Bruce stepped away from being one of the best CEOs in the global airline industry and moved to China to teach English to refugees. That may not be the same move you make, but the impulse is the same: responding to a restless heart and pursuing a new season of fulfillment. The sense of restlessness that prompted Bruce to step away from being the best of the best prompted him also to pursue something that gave him an even deeper sense of purpose.

A sense of restlessness can creep up on anyone. So why do we so often try to fit "new wine into old wineskins," as Jesus put it, instead of respecting the new vintage (Mark 2:22)? The answer is obvious: change is hard, and so we fear it.

As we move from the discernment to the anticipation phase of transition, we become filled with a confusing combination of positive and negative feelings. This is why the change feels even harder than it may be; our minds are trying to make sense of the mixed signals we pick up consciously and subconsciously. Our confidence level drops, and we begin to anticipate the many challenges the change will require. It is at this moment that we most need to remain level-headed and remind ourselves that this is the usual way God carries us through the changes of life.

# 2

# STANDING OUTSIDE

## WHY CHANGE
## HURTS YOUR HEAD

*There is nothing like looking,*
*if you want to find something.*
*You certainly usually find something,*
*if you look, but it is not always quite*
*the something you were after.*

J. R. R. TOLKIEN

At root, change means the partial or total abandonment of
the norms, safeties, and patterns of behavior that make our lives
manageable. Decision-making is mentally taxing, so we tend to
replace assessments and evaluations with automatic reactions
and instinctive habits whenever we can. Change entails losing familiar crutches that we lean on. If every day were our first day on
the job, or if every time we drove to work, we had to concentrate
on the map directing our travel, we would eventually wear out.
This is also why vacations to new places, especially international

ones, can be exhausting, even if they are a pleasure. The human endocrine system produces adrenaline, which gives us extra energy and focus on these "first day" or "first time" events. But the body cannot tolerate a steady supply of adrenaline. This is what causes hypertension and heart palpitations. Eventually, we move to a more stable state, but before then we must pass through the *anticipation* phase of transitions.

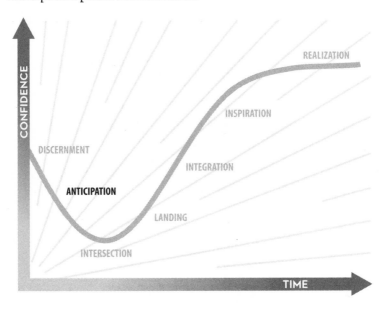

## SYSTEM ONE AND SYSTEM TWO

The preference for the easily navigated, familiar environment is explained by the difference between our two modes of thinking, which behavioral economist Daniel Kahneman has called "system one" and "system two." *System one* is automatic, subconscious, and takes little to no effort to use.[1] It is, for instance, used for identifying the location of sounds, or deciding which of two objects is closer to us. If I asked you what one plus two equals, you would only need system one to arrive at the correct answer.

*System two* is very different. It is the process by which we think slowly and deliberately to calculate and produce answers to difficult questions. Any response that is not auto-

> At root, change means the partial or total abandonment of the norms, safeties, and patterns of behavior that make our lives manageable.

matic makes use of system two. Focusing on a project at work or remembering where we first met someone require system-two thinking because they entail the processing of information that is not immediately known. If I were to ask you to solve for x: 1,389 = 237x, you would likely be able to give me an answer after some time, but it would require effortful calculation.

System one exists to make our lives easier and more manageable. We coast through much of our day with system one's automatic responses to known questions. It forms the mental shortcuts that help us get along without much effort. It allows us to ration our mental energy so we can save it for the more taxing questions as they come along.

When the automation of system one is lost because of changes in our lives, it is replaced by system two. This is the case even for small changes. I once asked a student who worked in my office what he considered the hardest thing about moving to college. His answer surprised me: "Having to pick what to wear each morning." He had come from a school that required a uniform every day; he had never needed to think about what he would wear or try to remember how long it had been since he had worn a particular outfit. The burden of choosing what to wear each day is a minor issue, but it demonstrates a larger point: all environmental changes, no matter how small, entail a transfer of responsibilities from system one to system two. A *complete* change of environment (like going to college) is so difficult because little can be done without system-two thinking. In your first week of classes, you have to actively remind yourself of when your classes are, where they meet, and the names of your professors. On top of that, you have to present yourself in socially acceptable ways to myriad new acquaintances. Until all this becomes routine, it demands additional mental energy. The same applies when we start a new job. Remembering all our coworkers' names is mentally taxing until it no longer is.

This is why change hurts your head. The option to relax a little and fall back on default actions is not available because in transitions there are no default actions yet—not until we establish our new patterns and ways of life.

## OVERCOMING OVERCAUTION

By nature, we humans are risk averse. The unknown makes us wary, not only because we want to avoid using too much system two but also because we don't want to die while doing it. Our earliest ancestors stuck to the paths they knew and stayed in a group rather than wandering around and getting eaten. Those who were more curious than cautious did not live long enough to become our ancestors.

A moderate dose of caution is healthy as a survival mechanism, but too much can keep us from successfully passing through open doors. I remember a conversation I had with Tom Tierney on this subject. Tom is the founder of the Bridgespan Group, an industry-leading firm that specializes in nonprofit consulting. Bridgespan exists to help people help others by maximizing the positive social impact of nonprofit organizations. Tom himself was leading a successful life in the private sector before he began the more civic-minded Bridgespan. He credits much of his success now to an early hinge moment in his life when he decided to check his caution and take a healthy risk.

When he was applying for a job right out of college in California, he did not even own a suit jacket for the interview. After a few minutes, his interviewer told him that they would like to offer him a job . . . in Algeria. Tom did not

> A moderate dose of caution is healthy as a survival mechanism, but too much can keep us from successfully passing through open doors.

even know where Algeria was, but he was excited by the new venture, so he took the job. The experience and the people he met working in Algeria for two years in his early twenties permanently altered his trajectory for the better. It takes a lot of willpower to overcome the natural caution you might feel at the prospect of moving across the world for an entry-level job. At first glance, that move might come across as foolhardy. However, taking risks like that (especially in your younger years) can be instrumental in determining your future. Hesitation at the prospect of major life transitions is normal, and wisdom should always prevail. But the data suggests that we humans may be *overly* cautious—to our detriment.

Dr. Steven Levitt of the University of Chicago conducted a relatively simple but illuminating study on major life decisions and happiness. He studied people who were contemplating a significant life change but were unsure about following through. The sorts of changes considered ranged from moves to new jobs to new romantic relationships. At the end of an online questionnaire, a virtual coin was "tossed." The results served as the answer generator to the question the participants were grappling with. If the coin landed on heads, it meant "yes, you should make this change." If it landed on tails, it meant, "no, you shouldn't." People were not required to follow through one way or another, of course, and they were surveyed twice again, two months and six months later.

Levitt found two counterintuitive insights about how we make decisions. Those for whom the coin landed on heads, indicating that they *should* alter the status quo, were much more likely to actually do it than were the tails group. This suggests that we are often more cautious than we need to be when considering a new move; sometimes it only takes a little confirmation to nudge us across the threshold. Even more interesting, however, is that those in the heads group who *did* make the change reported higher levels of happiness six months later than those who chose not to make the change.[2] So we are overcautious in our decision-making, but we end up happier after we change our circumstances.

Now, I'm not advocating making big life decisions based on a coin toss. And a sense of restlessness is not the same as anxiety or angst, which might have negative causes that need to be addressed. But if you find yourself feeling restless from within an otherwise contented state, that sentiment in itself may be all the indication you need to make a change. If you find yourself feeling that restlessness, you are blessed. It means that you have been afforded the benefit of time to plan the date and means of your transition.

## PLANNING VERSUS PREDICTING

Determining the "when" of a transition is always difficult, and there are more factors to consider than I can list here. Yet it's the sheer number of relevant variables that makes having some sort of plan so indispensable. The obvious benefit of long-term planning for change is that you have more options. Before the pen touches the paper, there is no theoretical limit to how the characters in a novel might develop. The same goes for us at the start of a life transition.

The closer we are to the fruition of our expectations, however, the more reality will temper them. It is probably unrealistic to have the goal of owning your own successful business next week if you are currently a sophomore in college, but it is perfectly reasonable to set that as a goal for fifteen years from now. This is the creative benefit of future planning: we can envision with relative freedom and minimal limitations the reality we would like best. This freedom is diminished as the time frame shrinks between *now* and *one day*. But at the moment of planning, the freedom is immense. And this ought to inspire us to dream away.

But the downside of future-casting when compared to more immediate planning is that it is notoriously inaccurate. The truth is that very few of us end up doing exactly what it is we set out to do. Even more discouraging is the fact that less than 30 percent of working Americans who attended college are working in a job related to their major.[3] This is not so much a problem with *planning* but with *predicting*. Sometimes we think we know exactly what we will be doing, but more often than not, our forecasts are wrong.

Predictions are a natural part of thinking about the future, but they are also—fundamentally—liabilities. History is rife with examples of failed predictions. Take, for example, the Beatles' audition at Decca Studios in 1962. The relatively new band came in and played fifteen songs for the studio staff. Several days later, the band was informed that even though they sounded great, they would not be receiving a contract because the executives felt that "guitar groups are on the way out."[4] Big mistake. Hindsight is 20/20, so perhaps we could forgive Decca for the millions of dollars they lost. But this cautionary tale, like all missed opportunities, serves as a powerful warning against putting too much stock into any given prediction. Basing major life decisions on *predictions* is dangerous but basing them on *plans* is a different thing altogether. Long-term life plans can be intensely useful guides. The key is not to rely solely on one plan that depends on one particular prediction, no matter how guaranteed the outcome might seem right now.

Dave Evans at Stanford is one of the premier experts on the practice of life planning. A product designer by trade, he cofounded EA, one of the world's largest video game companies. But he has become more famous for the program he coteaches at Stanford on helping students design their lives. Dave has taught the course to thousands of students, and I had the privilege of sitting down with him to better understand just how he goes about it. He talked at length about the philosophies that undergird the approach most undergraduates take to life planning. He noted the typical understanding of a dichotomy between secular and sacred. He says that most people have a bunch of unwritten rules in their head about what God is and is not allowed to take interest in. This separation narrows the scope of what they think about theologically. A more holistic view of work and vocation recognizes that the secular workplace is not outside of God's purview. Rather, the scope of matters (including careers and workplaces) that God cares about is vast. Dave told me that for most students, once he is able to persuade them to this way of thinking, their sense of their future possibilities goes from "the size of a checkerboard to the size of a football field." In short, the first step toward making a plan is to expand the range of possible vocational paths available so that we can view the world more like God does. Everything we do can be sacred.

One of the more intriguing aspects of what Dave teaches involves something that he calls the Odyssey Plan,[5] which involves simply projecting a five-year plan for yourself and then describing how that plan measures on a few scales like coherence and likability. The brilliance of the technique is that students produce not one but three distinct plans for the next five years. The first is a standard plan; the second is a backup plan; the third is one with no restrictions on resources (like money). The point is simple: "There is no one idea for your life. There are many lives you could live happily and productively."[6] This is a fundamental truth about planning for transitions in life. There are always many doors before you, which you might choose to open or close. There is never only *one* correct choice.

In some ways, we have to adopt the mindset of a serial entrepreneur—namely, a willingness to try out different options and to take some risks in our own life planning. One of the most impressive examples of this over the last decade is Praxis, which Dave Blanchard cofounded. Based in New York City, Praxis seeks to advance a faith-centered approach to starting new ventures called "redemptive entrepreneurship." Through mentorships that

Praxis brokers, practical instruction they provide to aspiring and experienced entrepreneurs, and supportive communities they foster around the country, Praxis catalyzes the creativity of Christians who want to build faith-inspired businesses and nonprofits that make a positive difference. In many ways, Blanchard himself embodies the Praxis ethos. A millennial who earned degrees from Babson and Northwestern, he launched Praxis in 2011 after successfully launching two companies and serving as a principal designer at IDEO, the nation's leading design-thinking firm. He wanted to help Christians not only get a job but actually create jobs for others and in the process contribute to the growth and well-being of the wider culture.

According to the Kauffman Foundation, more than half of millennials want to start a new venture or be part of a startup.[7] We are living in what Blanchard calls "an entrepreneurial age."[8] Connecting the creative impulse of our time with the desire to make a difference in the world is one of the ways we can respond to the anticipation phase of transition. Explore new possibilities with an entrepreneur's energy. Apply design-thinking to your own future by trying out a possible direction, testing it, and then making improvements. That's the benefit of shadowing someone on the job or completing an internship as you figure out a possible career turn. And get lots of feedback from others. When you are thinking about marrying someone, nothing can clarify your thinking better than hearing the perspectives of those who know and love you best.

Of course, the number of doorways available to you will change over time. Remember that the farther away you are from a hinge moment, the more options you retain. As time moves forward, your once-distant transitions will gradually become anticipatable changes. Your flexibility on the date of the change will diminish, until the day you have planned for becomes certain enough for you to circle it on your calendar with a red Sharpie. At any given moment, it is always possible that you may be forced through a door by floodwaters or an angry boss. These sudden changes throw wrenches into our plans, but they also provide opportunities for restructuring and renewal. And even in the future, when we have run out of red circles on our calendar, when we have no boss to fire us and our ten-year plans are twenty years old, it may be then that a sense of restlessness creeps into our life—calling us, nudging us to look for a new doorway and to consider what our next hinge moment has to offer.

## DON'T LET FEAR STEAL YOUR FUTURE

The Old Testament tells a poignant story reflecting the anticipation phase of transition. As the Hebrew people were approaching the Promised Land, Moses sent twelve operatives to scout out the land. They were hopeful but nervous.

> The LORD spoke to Moses, saying, "Send men to spy out the land of Canaan, which I am giving to the people of Israel. From each tribe of their fathers you shall send a man, every one a chief among them." So Moses sent them from the wilderness of Paran, according to the command of the LORD . . . and said to them, "Go up into the Negeb and go up into the hill country, and see what the land is, and whether the people who dwell in it are strong or weak, whether they are few or many, and whether the land that they dwell in is good or bad, and whether the cities that they dwell in are camps or strongholds, and whether the land is rich or poor, and

whether there are trees in it or not. Be of good courage and
bring some of the fruit of the land." (Numbers 13:1-3, 17-20 ESV)

The goal of the mission was simple and clear. God had already told
the people that they were going to inherit the land. The decision
had already been made but they needed to scope out the possibilities. Would there be good soil in which to grow food? Did they
need a plan of attack, or could they waltz in and take over the
place? Most of the spies returned with a frightening picture:

At the end of forty days, they returned from spying out the
land. And they came to Moses and Aaron and to all the con-
gregation of the people of Israel. . . . And they told him, "We
came to the land to which you sent us. It flows with milk and
honey, and this is its fruit. However, the people who dwell in
the land are strong, and the cities are fortified and very large.
And besides, we saw [giants] there." (Numbers 13:25-28 ESV)

Ten of the spies reported that the people currently guarding the
promised land were "giants" compared to the Hebrews, and fear
spread throughout the nation. Only Joshua and Caleb stuck with
the plan, assuring the people of Israel that the Lord would be with
them and would give them victory against the giants. The people
grumbled against Moses and their fears intensified. Because of
their lack of faith, the Lord barred them from entering the
Promised Land for another forty years. Fear had stolen their future.

The move was already *happening*. Why, then, did the ten spies
spend so much energy thinking up reasons to turn around? It was
prudent to find out where the food in the land grew and where the
inhabitants were located. But there was no reason to invent stories
of giants, trying to scare everyone back to Egypt.

When you scout out a plan of action for your transition somewhere, focus on the milk and honey rather than the supposed "giants." There may be giants, but that does not mean they will defeat you. And they certainly should not dissuade you from following the Lord's leading. There is no one on earth who can subvert the call of God.

I interact with countless high school students each year who are in the midst of a serious transition: deciding which college to attend. Today, there are two million *fewer* college students in American than there were eight years ago.[9] There are several reasons for this, but the response from colleges has been obvious. They are more actively engaged in persuading students to attend their school than ever before. They are doing everything they can to get prospective students to believe their school is precisely what they are looking for. The quality of programming of admissions days has necessarily improved, the care given by admissions staff has increased, and the cultivation of a positive image is managed much more closely. Colleges are not being deceptive, but they are being deliberate in how they market themselves.

As a result, I talk with a lot of students about their college decision-making process. The truth is that many schools *look* similar in their presentation and marketing. And I certainly encourage students to visit any college they are seriously considering attending, but that is not enough. To know what the school is really like you have observe the institution in moments when not everything is curated for you.

The best advice I give to high school students looking at a certain university is simple: spend a weekend, or at least a Friday or Saturday night, on the campus. Get to know the campus culture away from the watchful eyes of the recruiting team and apart from the standard campus tour. Eat the food the students eat and walk the halls they walk. See students in unguarded moments and learn about the college's "hidden curriculum" (that is, everything that is more caught than taught). The concept dates back to Émile Durkheim, the father of modern sociology. He argued that in the school setting—but way beyond the classroom—there were "a host of obligations" expected of students that help them become part of the school's culture and inculcate a spirit of discipline.[10]

This hidden curriculum is everywhere, both in the college classroom and in the workplace. It informs what you do and who you do it with. It provides you with expectations about your behavior and that of others and it defines what sort of person you will be influenced to become while you are there. You pick it up from the posters on the wall and the music played in the residence halls. It includes the norms about dating and student-faculty interactions, and the traditions that come to define the university. This applies not just to higher education; every institution has its own form of a hidden curriculum. And learning as much as you can about it *before* you begin your transition there can only help you.

## THE FRUITS AND FORTRESSES OF THE LAND

When the Hebrews sent their scouts into the land of Canaan, Moses told them to bring back some fruit from the land. This may seem like an odd request to us, but it was a critically important matter. The type and abundance of the fruit they retrieved would give the Hebrews an idea of what kind of land they were inheriting. The request for a report on the presence of towns and strongholds would round out the picture and prepare them for whatever incursions they might experience. The kind of transition they were going through is vastly different than the kind we typically go through today, but a similarity remains: It is good to know what the land is made of and who lives there. To these Bronze-Age Hebrews, the land was held together by fruit and strongholds. Our "new territories" today are held together by major institutions and large organizations. As such, they deserve our scrutiny and prayerful consideration.

Institutions have been part of society ever since God established the first family in Genesis. Today they permeate every aspect of our lives through work, school, government, and our social worlds. Simply put, an institution is something that organizes patterns of behavior. Gordon College is an institution, but so are cooking and football. They represent ways we order our lives, and each entails a set of rules and roles, beliefs and behaviors that we master and then pass along to others. Institutions simplify our complex lives, and they depend on a measure of trust and confidence in them.

Today, however, trust in major institutions is approaching an all-time low. The Pew Research Center finds that nearly half of all American young adults are "low trusters." By this they mean that they "are more likely to see others as selfish, exploitative and untrustworthy." This lack of interpersonal trust translates into low trust in certain institutions and their leaders. For example, only 50 percent of the young adults surveyed said that they trust religious leaders, compared to 70 percent of respondents who were over the age of fifty. Only about a third of young adults expressed confidence in business leaders or elected officials. This is bad because these leaders are stand-ins for the institutions they represent. When institutions and leaders cannot generate public trust and confidence, the vast majority of young adults (73 percent) come to the conclusion that most people "just look out for themselves."[11]

It is difficult to evaluate the fruit and fortresses of a possible future land when we trust institutions so little. And yet our well-being depends on overlapping networks of trust. People who have a productive, meaningful life find ways to trust and to be trustworthy. This sense of trust means a reduced sense of anxiety, which helps them make better decisions about their future and create positive opportunities for themselves as well as their families and friends. Political scientist Hugh Heclo puts it this way: "Current decisions are made with a continuing awareness that you are enjoying the fruits of something be-longing to predecessors and successors. Therefore, while change is inevitable, the recognition of its implications is em-bedded in a strong appreciation for what has gone on before you were here and what will go on after you are gone."[12]

> People who have a productive, meaningful life find ways to trust and to be trustworthy.

As political thinkers such as Robert Putnam have convincingly shown, institutions and the rela-tionships they make possible are the glue that holds us together; they provide sources of meaning. This is true not only for us but for the places we call home as well. When you move to a new place, you will find dozens of institutions such as schools, churches, social clubs, and community gathering spots. When you start a new job, you are joining at least one new institution. When you head off to college, not only is your university an institution in its own right but the school itself will be full of countless others in the form of teams, clubs, and extracurricular groups.

To succeed in your transitions, you have to look before you leap. This means doing your due reconnaissance, scouting out the area's "fruits and fortresses" (institutions and organizations). Yet watch out for fear and anxiety, which will creep in to steal your future or at least to cause such distrust that you are not able to move to the next phase, which is found only at the meeting place of your old life and your new, of your past and your future.

# 3

# STRADDLING THE THRESHOLD

## THE SPACE BETWEEN SPACES

*For years I have looked ahead,*
*searching for holy places down the road*
*and trying to reach them as soon as possible.*
*Now I believe instead that this ground is sacred,*
*and wherever I stand this moment is holy.*

JUDITH E. SMITH

Before vampires were gorgeous, misunderstood characters in heartthrob novels and movies, they were something much more sinister. To the people of medieval and early modern eastern Europe, they were a legitimate threat. The modern reader will no doubt be familiar with popular measures against vampires, such as a wooden stake, garlic, and a crucifix. But there is an even more powerful ward against in them in the oldest traditions: not inviting them in.

The pre-Hollywood vampires from the folklore of the Balkans and eastern Europe were dangerous creatures, but they had to play by certain rules. One such rule was that they could not cross the threshold of a home until they had been welcomed in. In fact, for the premoderns, the protective power of the threshold extended to all manner of evil beings. In Johann Goethe's *Faust,* for instance, the demon Mephistopheles was likewise stopped at the threshold until invited in. Evil is repeatedly kept at bay by thresholds. Today these concepts may seem quaint, even incomprehensible. But to our premodern ancestors, these traditions were rooted in an undeniable truth: the threshold has power.

The daily lives of people in the ancient and medieval worlds were steeped in symbolism. To us a threshold is a piece of wood beneath a door frame; to them it marked spatial delineation. It was a barrier so strong that it kept at bay the demons of hell. So important was this threshold that there were priests in the temple in Israel who were called "keepers of the threshold." In 2 Kings, we read about such men who worked at the temple entry points and who gathered donations and oversaw the sacred vessels. More generally, these priests were there to maintain a separation between the sacred and the profane because there was a common understanding that the threshold had extraordinary importance in delineating these spaces. So thresholds have mattered for a long time.

As we reach the point between our old and new lives—between being single and married or leaving one job and starting another—we find ourselves straddling a threshold, existing in the space between spaces. Here we encounter the *intersection* phase of a transition. Because of the inherently insecure nature of this stage in which we are betwixt and between, our confidence reaches its lowest ebb and our connections to others (in both our old and new places) are weakest. With the fewest sources of support, we rely almost entirely on immediate family members, lifelong friends, and mentors to sustain us and help us navigate. And because self-doubt and second-guessing are most common in this phase, seeking their counsel and following their advice is among the most important things we can do.

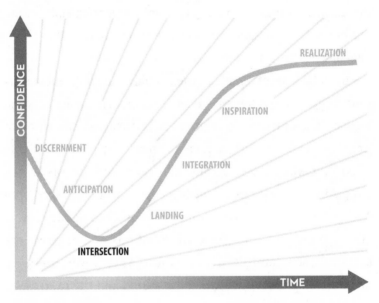

## STEP BOLDLY ACROSS

Joseph Campbell was one of the twentieth century's preeminent scholars of comparative mythology. His most famous work, *The Hero with a Thousand Faces*, popularized the concept of the hero's journey. The idea is that all of humanity's great hero stories repeat similar patterns. In short, the hero leaves the mundane and enters a world of supernatural beings and powers. He is helped by a mentor or guide, fights a decisive battle or resists temptation, descends into the underworld, emerges a changed person, and returns home with riches or powers. This cycle is recognizable in many noteworthy stories, including *The Epic of Gilgamesh, The Odyssey, The Lord of the Rings, The Wizard of Oz,* and the *Harry Potter* series. George Lucas himself made direct reference to Campbell's influence on *Star Wars*. In this nearly ubiquitous cycle of tropes, the beginning stages of the hero's journey typically feature an easily identifiable threshold crossing. The hero leaves the safety of his home and sets out for danger and adventure.

Bob Mazzuca served for many years as Chief Scout Executive (read CEO) of the Boy Scouts of America. In his role, he was responsible for overseeing an organization that serves over two million active scouts. He recounted for me how he stepped over a significant threshold when he left home for college. He was the first member of his family (of seven siblings) to graduate from high school, let alone go to college. His father had immigrated from Italy and had always impressed on him the value of higher education if he could be admitted somewhere. If Odysseus was the archetypal hero for the national story of Greece, the penniless son of an immigrant on his way off to college is the archetypical hero in America's national story. Mazzuca put it this way:

> When I left for school, I'll never forget, my dad . . . reached in his pocket and gave me a twenty-dollar bill. That's all he could—he could not afford twenty bucks, but he gave me twenty bucks. And I just headed off to San Luis Obispo, which is about three-and-a-half hours away. It might have been on the moon as far as I was concerned, because I had never been away from home. It was a real adventure, a real adventure.

As the president of a college, I see hundreds of students arrive each fall who are just beginning this new chapter. They come from different backgrounds, different parts of the world, and on the surface, they are quite distinct from one another. But they are all the same in one regard: they have each just entered a new season of life. Their parents will keep a bed for them at home, but it is never quite the same when they return on breaks. The place is familiar, yet it is different because *they* are different. It is (hopefully) still a place of love and care, but it is no longer "home" the way it was when they were children.

When I address the new families at orientation each fall, they are typically surprised at one piece of advice I always give the students: do not go home for the fall break in October. Thanksgiving will come soon enough, and there is value in embracing their *new* "home." This transition can be startling, but as students commit to stepping boldly into it, it need not be stifling.

Of course, crossing the threshold can be *frightening* and *isolating.* The frightening aspects of the unknown are compounded by the mass of new sensory information, which requires your brain to run system-two thinking on all cylinders. The isolation can creep in during the time between the loosening of ties with old friends and peers and the weaving of new ones with new people. It's crucial to make new connections with others in your life stage; you can meet them around the neighborhood, in your new workplace, at playdates for your children (if you are transitioning into parenting), in your dorm, or even in common interest groups online.

However, *mentors* are just as important as peers, and even more so when crossing a threshold. Indeed, they may be the most important resource in this phase of our lives.

## THE ROLE OF A MENTOR

In our epic stories, the character of the mentor is needed precisely because home is cozy and warm, and what is out there in the great beyond is less so. The mentor urges us toward greatness through risk-taking and threshold-crossing. There is no start to Bilbo's journey without Gandalf, or Luke's without Obi-Wan. Dante cannot pass over the threshold into the Inferno without Virgil, and Dorothy cannot set foot on the yellow brick road until Glinda shows her the way.

Mentors, by definition, have already walked where you are about to step, and they've had time to process the lessons they learned along the way, so a peer who gives good advice might be a great asset, but that person isn't a mentor. True mentors can be invaluable sources of advice and direction when you need them, taking some of the edge off the hard decision-making early on in a new "space" because you can lean on their expertise where yours may be lacking.

Mentoring relationships are not merely casual friendships between two people; there is more intentionality to them than that. Jennifer Mueller at the Wharton School of the University of Pennsylvania put it this way: "It has to be long term . . . with frequent meetings, not arbitrary. You cannot just meet to talk about 'stuff' three times a year." These relationships are meant to be productive: goals are named and pursued; beneficial habits established and reinforced. Ideally, these relationships can enrich your life and set you up for greater

> True mentors can be invaluable sources of advice and direction when you need them.

success than you would otherwise have. In a business setting, employees who have mentors earn more, are better socialized into the workplace culture, feel less stressed, and are promoted more rapidly than their peers without mentors.[1]

Researchers at Johns Hopkins University conducted a study on persistence rates for college freshmen in the United States. Persistence is the rate by which freshmen who arrive in the fall choose to continue at the college at least into their next semester. The research team found that perception of mentorship was one of the two strongest correlating factors with freshmen persistence (the other being college self-efficacy, the belief in one's ability to handle college tasks).[2] Surprisingly, factors such as grade point average, standardized test scores, and socioeconomic status had no correlation at all. This study demonstrates not only the extraordinary value a mentor can add to a life but also how important it is to get one early on during a major transition. To the graduating high school student on his or her way to college, this may seem a daunting task. But as someone who has spent over a decade researching the topic, I have picked up some valuable tips.

First, ask the Lord to lead you to a mentor. I prayed for several months before meeting George Gallup (whose father started the Gallup Poll). When we first met for coffee, I did not know he would have such a profound impact on my life—eventually encouraging me to undertake a doctorate in sociology, giving me the chance to write multiple books with him, and opening up an entirely new vocation in my life. But looking back I can see that our first connection over coffee was the beginning of God's answer to my prayer for a mentor.

And you don't have to find the "Best. Mentor. Ever." Simply jump in by picking three people who have walked where you're interested in going and ask each one of them to meet with you one-on-one. (This is also a great way to get to know the coolest coffeehouses in your area, so . . . bonus.) Things will develop naturally from there, and you will gradually know if the fit is right. I know a student at Gordon who asked several more-senior people to coffee on his very first day as a freshman. The relationships he made then helped him kickstart his college career, and he ended up serving as student-body president by his junior year. This scattershot method does not always work out as well as it did for this student, but it is a great way to start. If you are struggling to identify promising candidates, look around at church and in your community. Find someone who appears to be living a life that you're interested in exploring (either in terms of career and vocation or perhaps in terms of life-and-work balance or godly character). Then, find ways to connect with different people, realizing that not everyone you may be interested in meeting will necessarily have the time or interest to respond. But in God's providence, if you remain patient and gently persistent, I expect you will be surprised how often the Lord will connect you with others who can become helpful influences in your life.

Second, be sure to keep in touch with any mentors you had in your last setting. There's a traditional Girl Scout campfire song that says, "Make new friends, but keep the old. One is silver and the other gold." This couldn't be more accurate when it comes to mentors. Just because you are "moving on" to a new phase of life doesn't mean that you should leave behind your old mentors (you absolutely should not). In fact, these people can be some of the most useful mentors for you at the onset of a transition; they already know you better than anyone in the new space could. With modern technology, there is no reason for you to lose contact just because of geographical distance. Emailing regularly is a great first step, and planning to get together when you are next back in town is even better.

Finally, find reasons to stay in regular contact with both groups of advisers—old and new. Keep notes on everyone's birthdays and anniversaries. Send holiday cards that are hand signed. Keep tabs on your mentors' accomplishments and milestones, and congratulate them. Follow their accounts on social media and comment on their posts. Of course, there is a big difference between sycophancy and friendliness; intentionality need not be insincere. The goal is not to flatter but to connect, even in little ways. Your attempts at staying connected should communicate that you value this person being in your life, and for that reason you don't want to lose touch.

## DON'T BURN YOUR SHIPS

Spanish explorer Hernán Cortés famously "burned the ships" when he landed in the New World of South America. He and his men were on a mission of colonization for the crown of Spain, and Cortés made it clear that there was only one way for their expedition to go: forward. Mutiny with the goal of returning home was no longer an option. According to Virgil, Aeneas did the same thing when he landed in Italy. Elimination of the way back home ensured everyone was fully committed because the options were now limited—to one.

Life is not like that. It is seldom a good idea to "burn your ships." Of course, I can think of *some* pathways that should be permanently cut off, especially when it comes to unhealthy or immoral situations. In those cases, yes: Flush the pills. Block the number. Cancel the channel. But never cut important ties to people or organizations simply because of your own irritation, ennui, or short-term bad experience. Despite confidence in your own predictions, always leave open the possibility of an about-face and return to base.

To make sure a return journey is always theoretically available when you transition out of a space (a job, a school, even a romantic relationship), do so with grace. Resist the temptation to tell your boss what you *really* think of the company you are leaving. He or she may be a reference for you later. Do not drop all your friendships when you head off to college. Those people may be lifelong friends if you nurture those connections. And as for old boyfriends or girlfriends, watch your tone when you talk to others about the breakup, especially on social media. Slandering your ex might make your next potential date afraid of being a future victim of your ire.

> Never cut important ties to people or organizations simply because of your own irritation, ennui, or short-term bad experience.

In the same vein, be careful also that your ships don't fall into disrepair. Be considerate and thoughtful of others who have given you their time, mentoring, or funding. Say "thank you" more times than you say "please." Write handwritten notes to teachers, co-workers, or friends who have been especially good to you in your old space. These sorts of gestures not only engender a fondness that can be helpful later; they are just simply the right thing to do when saying good-bye. I'll be clear here: *nothing good will ever come of burning your relational ships.* Remember, fortunes turn quickly; you never know who will be your boss one day.

## BECOMING BILINGUAL

Each neuron in the cerebral cortex of a newborn's brain has about 2,500 synapses. By age three, a toddler has approximately 15,000 synapses per neuron, which is more than twice that of the typical adult. During the years between childhood and adulthood, our brains delete old connections through a process known as "synaptic pruning." Those connections that are activated most frequently are preserved and strengthened; those that are not maintained get removed. As a result, early exposure to ideas or concepts can create additional neural pathways in the human brain, which, if reinforced, can become information highways in our minds, making it easier to connect supplementary knowledge for years to come.

My twin daughters, Emily and Caroline, started learning Spanish around age four; their comprehension and accents far exceed anything my wife or I might be able to achieve as adult learners. Their fluency depends in part on the plasticity of their brains when they were first exposed to the unique sounds of the Spanish language. Not only have they been able to do what is difficult for most adults, but they are doing it with two languages *simultaneously*. My girls aren't superhuman. They are just kids. That's how amazing young people are!

Multicultural and multilingual people regularly experience the limbo that the rest of us feel during seasons of transition. They can do a similarly amazing thing: move between two worlds like natives of both, recalibrating themselves appropriately. This valuable skill is what anthropologists and linguists refer to as *code-switching*.

Veronica Biggins rose up through the ranks at Bank of America before being recruited to the Clinton White House as assistant to the president and director of presidential personnel. She often found herself translating portions of her experience as an African American woman in largely White workplace environments. When we sat down to talk about her journey, she told of a time when she was coaching a younger African American gentleman who was very good at his job but continually received mediocre feedback from clients. Biggins' colleagues could not figure what the problem was and thought he needed to leave the firm. She decided to step in and see if she could learn anything. After she described the feedback clients were providing on his performance, he replied directly, "My grandma told me never to look a White person in the face." Now, understand, this was not something happening in the early twentieth century; it occurred in our lifetime. It's hard to believe that kind of mindset might be keeping back a young Black executive, but that was precisely the case. Biggins understood his background (and the context of his grandmother's advice), and she not only saved his job but also helped him learn how to adjust to his new role.

Just like this young man, you might not understand at first the subtleties of multiple cultural settings, but you can still learn to code-switch. In fact, you do it every day. It occurs when you're talking to someone professionally and use less personal terms than you would with your friends. You do it when you don't use five-syllable words when explaining something to a toddler. Whenever you change your tone, language, or mannerisms to better suit the current moment, you are code-switching.

This is analogous to the code-switching we all perform as we progress through various stages of transition. We begin to "prune" away the automatic, subconscious habits of our old space and pick up for the first time the novel ways of thinking unique to our new one. In fact, research suggests that learning to switch back and forth between "codes" (modes of reasoning, speaking, and the like) strongly impacts our ability to solve problems and think efficiently in general.[3]

My Gordon College colleague Susan Bobb suggests that the presence of "cognates" between two languages affects the way we think about them both.[4] A cognate is a word that is related to a word of similar appearance and meaning in another language. For example, the Spanish word *flamenco* means "flamingo." English speakers learning that word in Spanish usually assimilate it with confidence because of its familiar spelling.

When we make transitions in life and encounter new inputs, finding things that *look* similar to what we knew in our old space is a shortcut, helping us adapt to the new environment. The most interesting finding of Bobb's research is not that bilingual individuals were able to make these connections but that even people who had just begun to learn the new language built up this ability quickly.

So when you find yourself learning something entirely new—like at the beginning of a transition—keep an eye out for what looks familiar. Treat any new space you move into as a new language you have to learn. Some things will be entirely foreign, and you will need to start from scratch with those. But it is likely there will be many things which, upon closer inspection, are similar

> When we make transitions in life and encounter new inputs, finding things that *look* similar to what we knew in our old space is a shortcut, helping us adapt to the new environment.

to ways of doing things back in your old life. For example, a family that used to pay weekly visits to a nursing home to visit a dying family member should continue the practice of getting together during that same time each week, even after the beloved family member passes away. Maintaining the continuity of regular family gatherings will assist the family in grieving the loss and begin the process of adopting a new "normal" for their family life. Or if you love your church community but are forced to move to a new town because of work or other life changes, try to find a faith community that reminds you of your former church (similar people, similar worship style, and the like). The stability you gain from the familiar will provide a helpful ballast in the midst of so many other adjustments. And as you get to know your new town, your new workplace, or your new family situation, keep an eye out for other similarities with your former life. Cognitively speaking, the more points of continuity you can find, the easier your brain will be able to process the transition and the more contentment you will find during this phase.

## FAST CHANGE, SLOW TRANSITION

Dr. Shirley Tilghman served as the president of Princeton University for twelve years, leading the school through a season of expanded academic opportunities and increased accessibility for students who could not afford to attend. She and I spoke about the shift she made from faculty member to president. The number one thing that stood out was that upon her inauguration—a fixed moment in time—she immediately had to adjust to the ways people viewed her differently. All of a sudden her mere attendance at an event was enough to warrant a great deal of gratitude from the host. Frustratingly, she could no longer brainstorm ideas aloud for fear that people would take her viewpoints as mandates coming from the top.

The crossing of a threshold is like Tilghman's inauguration. The transfer of power took minutes, but the countless internal changes she had to make took months and even years. This process of overlapping fast *and* slow change can create in us a sort of double consciousness where we feel like part of the old space *and* the new, but not wholly at home in either. This is what is called liminal space.

The word *liminal* unsurprisingly derives from the Latin word for "threshold." Liminal spaces were of such importance to the Romans that they had a god just for them—Janus. He is the god of beginnings, transitions, and endings—and so naturally, also of travelers. He is always depicted as having two faces, which lets him simultaneously look forward into the future and backward into the past. He is, therefore, the embodiment of the double consciousness brought on by transitional periods. His veneration was so important that the Romans set in motion the annual, month-long homage that we know as January.

As we pass over thresholds from one season of life into the next, we can feel like Janus, with one face looking in each direction yet fully attentive to neither. This is the intersection phase of transitions. If you are fortunate enough, you will be granted time to adjust—to learn and grow accustomed to the new place in the premier days and weeks across the threshold. First-year college students can go home on holidays, testing out their newfound habits and sensibilities in a more familiar setting. First-time parents can receive guidance and relief from the burdens of raising a newborn from their own parents and friends as they transition into a new phase of life with new priorities. The shock of a sudden relocation can be softened when old friends help you move, come visit you in your new town, and connect you with others they might know who live there already. In this way, people are able to gradually wean themselves off of their old life as they drink in the new one. So even when the move across the barrier must be instantaneous, having extra time for a gradual internal transition can make the whole ordeal easier.

Sometimes, however, transitions give us little time for internal adjustment. Shane Tedjarati is the president for global high growth regions at Honeywell, one of the world's largest companies. Honeywell produces everything from airplane parts to sporting goods, and Shane is part of the reason their stock has quintupled in the past fifteen years. But before he was a successful business mogul, Tedjarati was a refugee fleeing the Iranian revolution. Sensing the impending upheaval, his parents sent him overseas to Canada when he was just fourteen. Within a year, his country was in flames, his sister kidnapped, and he was marooned in Canada with no money, no contacts, and no understanding of the culture. He would not see his mother again for twenty years, and his family would never be fully reunited.

At the age of fifteen, he actually negotiated the release of his sister (who had been taken to Mexico) and brought her to Canada to live with him: "So I had to grow up. I went from fifteen to twenty-one overnight, in three months. I really had to become totally mature, you know," he recounted to me. "I have no youth. I was a child, and then I was an adult."

Although most of us will never make quite such a dramatic transition, this story illustrates just how quickly we might have to cross a threshold into a new place. Shane Tedjarati was ushered straight through the liminal space of adolescence and forced to reckon with the new realities not only of adulthood but also of a new country and new family situation. Traditional sources of support and comfort, including parents and even understanding the culture around him, disappeared in the blink of an eye. He was forced into a transition and through the liminal space in ways most of us never will be.

The liminal spaces that most of us experience can be difficult ones, but they are almost certainly better than not having that space at all (as Tedjarati experienced). Sure, the double consciousness can be exhausting, and the tendency to feel homeless is real. But rather than view the liminal space as a difficulty to be endured, view it as a blessing in your quest for maturity and expertise. Begin the crossing like Janus, with eyes in both directions —looking backward for support and with gratitude, and looking forward to new opportunities that wait on the other side.

Still today, thresholds are powerful symbols. They separate what was previously mundane from the world of new adventures and dangers beyond. Yet even those people who look before they leap must eventually leap, or else they find their open doorways have closed and become windows of what might have been. As Joseph Campbell described the threshold, "The powers that watch at the boundary are dangerous; to deal with them is risky; yet for anyone with competence and courage the danger fades."

# 4

# THE WELCOME MAT

## LANDING IN
## YOUR NEW SPACE

*You shall treat the stranger
who sojourns with you as the native
among you, and you shall love him as yourself,
for you were strangers in the land of Egypt:
I am the LORD your God.*

LEVITICUS 19:34 (ESV)

IN ENGLISH, both *guest* and *host* derive from the same root word. Originally that word, *ghosti*, referred to the complex and important relationship between a host and his or her guest. There were obligations and expectations that went both ways: hospitable conduct, expressions of gratitude, exchange of gifts, proper manners, and concern for a traveler's safety in a strange land.

Here in the United States, the phrase "Southern hospitality" conjures up an image of strangers welcomed to the dinner table with the biggest slice of pie reserved for them. But we've got nothing on other parts of the world where welcome-based duties run so deep that failing to treat a host or guest according to custom can cause scandal that impacts even future generations.

There will be plenty of times in your life when you will have the opportunity to serve as a host. But when you experience new transitions, when you cross a threshold into a new space, you become (albeit temporarily) a guest. This phase will not last forever; eventually, you'll feel more like a mainstay than a newcomer. As long as you are a guest, however, you should do what my Southern mom always said as I went out the door: Be on your best behavior, say "thank you" often, and don't do anything to embarrass our family.

## MAKING A GOOD FIRST IMPRESSION

After you have landed an offer at a new company, been accepted by a university, married into a new family, or begun some other new chapter of life, it can be tempting to *relax*. You deserve it, you'll tell yourself. After all, the people in charge of gatekeeping (human resources, admissions, your new spouse) have considered you worthy. They have seen your resume, called your references, okayed your application, or in the case of marriage, vowed "till death do us part." Even so, the task of winning over these people is far from complete. You should give as much thought and preparation to your first days in the new space as you gave to the deliberation process prior to the transition. *There is absolutely no substitute for a good first impression.*

The *landing* phase of a transition is filled with making impressions and forming opinions. Much of your time will be dominated by meeting new people, learning new routines, and establishing new patterns. Although you will be nervous about all the unknowns and eager to make friends and settle in, the landing stage is not nearly as scary as the liminal reality of the intersection phase. At this point, you've brought your adopted baby home, you've started the new job, or you've moved to your new house. Each interaction becomes an additional data point as you gain your bearings and start making sense of your new reality.

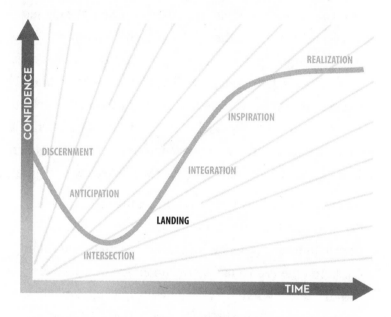

Humans have developed highly refined skills in facial recognition regarding intent and emotion. These skills developed originally to perceive danger or recognize ill intent in the faces of others before it was too late. Today these subconscious processes are generally used in more benign situations, but they are useful nonetheless. In fact, psychological research suggests that people consistently make subconscious assessments of the *trustworthiness* of others based on facial appearance. If you make a good impression initially, you may be more likely to earn yourself the benefit of the doubt should a conflict arise. If you don't engender trust early, however, others will be more likely to assign future blame to you—whether earned or not.[1]

Ideally, your transitions will go smoothly and the first few days in a new space will be filled with nothing but orientation and easy adjustment. Other times, for reasons well beyond your control, you may enter a new space in which the people are already suspicious of you. In times like these, it is even more important for you to make high-quality first impressions. When Dan Bartlett was serving as counselor to the president in 2005, he found himself two generations younger than his "peers" in a field that valued experience and the wisdom of elders. He looked and often felt fresh-faced and out of place. He recounted one of the early interactions he had with Donald Rumsfeld, then secretary of defense:

> We're all waiting outside the Oval Office, and there was some decision that there was clearly a split view of. And so it's Powell, Rumsfeld, Cheney, Rice, Hadley, myself, and Andy Card. And the President's on the phone in the Oval Office with the door closed, so we're all waiting, cooling our jets. But Rumsfeld had done his homework; he knew I was on one side, and not his, and so he turns to me, and says, "Danny"— and remember, this is the guy who was the youngest chief of staff, the youngest secretary of defense ever—and he goes, "Remind me how old you are?" And I go, "Well, Mr. Secretary, I'm thirty-four years old." "Good golly!" He's like, "I've got suits that are older than you, son!" It was kind of like, "Don't [mess] with me." And I said, without missing a beat, "Yes, Mr. Secretary, and this must be one of them." And everyone, Powell was like, "Ooh, Rummy, he got you back!"

The fact is that no matter your reputation where you came from, there will be people in your new space with negative expectations for you. (You will have to judge for yourself if the kind of jab Barlett took at Rumsfeld would be perceived in your new space as gutsy or insubordinate—best not to risk something like that until you're sure.) When you arrive already with a "negative score" like Barlett did, though, you'll need to come to terms with the fact that you're playing catch-up. Sometimes, like in baseball, you just have to suit up and play the position you've been assigned.

Often enough, common sense and a friendly attitude are enough to ingratiate yourself in your new space during your first few days. Being convivial and courteous to your new boss and peers will hopefully open up their minds to your positive qualities. Defer to the experience of others around

> Sometimes, like in baseball, you just have to suit up and play the position you've been assigned.

you; save your bright ideas until you understand the current state of affairs. In the meantime, be a good "guest." Do your best to remember names; make flashcards if you have to. Tell a (appropriate) joke; laugh at jokes made by others. Ask questions and display interest in the new people in your environment. From Dale Carnegie's classic, *How to Win Friends and Influence People*, comes the timeless advice that "you make more friends in two months by becoming interested in other people than you can in two years by trying to get other people to be interested in you."[2] Finally, believe it or not, *thousands* of peer-reviewed scholarly articles have been devoted to the topic of eye-contact and handshake proficiency. Make sure yours are spot-on to maximize others' perceptions of your care and conscientiousness.[3]

When you are a new spouse or a new hire, of course, you are unavoidably the center of attention. As a college freshman (or transfer student), though, you'll be anything but unique. In an environment where teachers and students have to make hundreds of first impressions and formulate early opinions of each other, shortcuts are taken by necessity. For new college students, then, I recommend not just getting the basic actions right, but also avoiding the mistake of *in*action. The first week—with its accommodating orientation leaders and lots of free time to acclimate— flies by in a flash, and then the guardrails come off and you have to hit the ground running. The best way to take advantage of these first few days of grace is to go out of your way to make connections with the people around you, especially potential mentors. Write emails to the professors in your major, asking each one to meet for a cup of coffee. (Trust me, professors are always looking for future protégés passionate about their field of study.) Find the organizations on campus that you think you would like to join and then identify some of their leaders. Offer to get them lunch sometime to talk about what it is they do and how they got there. With myriad new students just like you showing up at the same time, anything you can do to make yourself stand out (in a positive way) is a good thing.

When you do enter the workforce, remember what was emphasized earlier: positions are rarely ever exactly what anyone (employer or employee) anticipated. There will be things you are asked to do in your first weeks that will almost certainly be outside the scope of your official responsibilities. Success at an organization (promotions, raises, tenure) belongs to those who are willing to do things both above and below one's pay grade. If you complain early about having to do things that you feel are beneath you, I can promise your boss will never give you any opportunities that are above you. That kind of objection signals a lack of gratitude and maturity.

If a job is not exactly what you had expected or hoped, give it six months. Then, sit down with your boss and talk about responsibilities. Talk to him or her about what additional tasks (above or below) you are doing beyond the initial scope of your job description. If needed, ask your employer what they could see you doing there in the years to come. Employees who manage tasks and responsibilities in this way are far more likely to succeed than employees who start off with objections to what is asked of them. Resolving to check in at six months not only gives you the opportunity to make a good impression by gladly managing the tasks you are given in the first few months; it also gives you the chance to set yourself up to make an even better impression than your first.

When Don Willett was in his early thirties, President George W. Bush offered him a position as special assistant to the president as well as director of law and policy for a new government office focused on faith-based initiatives. Don and I spoke about his first few weeks in Washington, DC. He confessed that he had not been exactly thrilled with the position. He found the work meaningful, but he really had a judicial goal for his career that such a stint in DC would not necessarily advance. Nonetheless, he told me, when the president came knocking, he knew it was his duty to "salute smartly" and do the work. He had considered asking to serve instead in the White House Counsel's Office or the Department of Justice. But he chose instead to do without complaint the task he had been given.

Fast forward a couple decades. The Honorable Judge Don Willett has served several terms as a justice on the Texas Supreme Court and was appointed in 2016 as a judge on the United States Fifth Circuit Court of Appeals. His willingness to work in a position not immediately advancing his legal career created for him a good reputation for diligent work, which propelled him when he eventually returned to the Lone Star State. If he had complained to the White House about not being in the job of his dreams, he might have had a different trajectory. The fact is, sometimes the squeaky wheel gets the *boot*.

> The fact is, sometimes the squeaky wheel gets the *boot*.

## SECOND IMPRESSIONS AND MORE

In your early weeks and months in a new place, the changes that occur are unidirectional; the people and institutions that are already there will likely influence you—not the other way around. As you adapt and begin to contribute to your new space, however, you will grow in your potential effect. In the end, your second, third, and fourth (and so on) impressions on the people around you can become conduits for change. You will begin to create lasting modifications to the landscape of your new space, changes that will endure even after you are gone. Did you feel confused, underutilized, or overburdened when you first started your job? Well, now you might get to start making a difference in the systems that allowed that to happen.

Gail McGovern is the president of the American Red Cross. She has taught at Harvard Business School, served as a sales executive for Fidelity Investments, and programmed computers at AT&T.

She has had a sterling career as a businesswoman and has left her mark in many places. At AT&T in the early days of the internet, she often found herself in extremely male-dominated spaces. Back then, many companies still had different career tracks for men and women, with codified inequalities in the pay scale. She and I spoke about how she navigated that time in her life so successfully. She adapted to become successful in the environments in which she found herself. It was not always easy, but she did her job, ignored the naysayers, worked hard, and rose through the ranks.

You can bet that AT&T looked very different when she left than when she arrived. The day she became an officer there, only 5 percent of the company's officers were female. After her tenure, it was up to 30 percent, and it is even more balanced today. Mc-Govern is a prime example of impression building. She went to great lengths to fit in initially, leaving positive impression after positive impression. Today both she and the organizations she has touched are the better for it.

And then there is Clifton Wharton. The son of two American foreign service officers, Wharton traveled extensively as a child. He started at Harvard at age sixteen and went on to become the first African American president of a major US university. He later served as the CEO of a Fortune 100 company, and to round off his stellar career, he became the US deputy secretary of state under President Clinton.

When I asked him what distinguished his leadership, he gave a simple answer: "the shipboard tour." Growing up, he usually traveled from his parents' international assignments by ship, and he always loved to explore the vessel from stem to stern. As he got older, he continued a similar practice. When he became the president of Michigan State University, but before starting the job, he traveled to Lansing to interview every leader at the university. When he became the chancellor of the SUNY schools, he visited every one of the sixty-four campuses and met with all of the campus leaders within his first year on the job. And finally, when he became CEO of TIAA, one of the largest financial firms in the country, he spent his full first two days on the job walking every room of every floor of every building to greet every employee in person. For him, this was essential to figuring out how to lead the institutions most effectively. He found this the most straightforward way to succeed in the landing phase of a transition.

Often, the first days and weeks of a new job or new college experience are filled with moments of "what's next?" The shipboard tour could be a perfect way for you to spend some of your unassigned time in a new experience. The practice not only provides you with useful information early and quickly about "how things work around here," but it can catalyze new friendships and key relationships as you're finding your place in the new setting. Practicing it in each new context can become a helpful habit for long-term success. If your transition is one for employment, take the time to go around and shake everyone's hand. For new college students, go meet everyone on the floor of your residence hall. There are many other people around you looking for new friends just like you are.

And sometimes our expectations don't line up with the situation. According to a survey by Glassdoor (one of the country's largest job aggregators) as many as 61 percent of employees say that they found aspects of their new job differed from expectations they heard during the interview process.[4] The reasons for the gaps are typically not malicious intent on behalf of the employer, but rather communication mismatches between two parties. If you find yourself in this situation, follow three simple approaches: embrace, communicate, and recalibrate.

*Embrace* the new responsibilities you are being given and resist the temptation to reject added work in the first thirty days on the job. There is always a bit of sorting out of what the job entails, and you might be surprised how long it takes to get things done. Some assignments will take less time; some will take more. So, in the early days, welcome as much as you can of what you are told is part of the role.

During this time, however, you must *communicate*: stay in regular contact with your direct supervisor. You want your boss to know how you are spending your time, ensuring that she or he agrees with the time and energy allocations you are making.

As you approach ninety days on the job, this is a natural opportunity to *recalibrate* with your supervisor. Determine together if your role should keep or abandon certain aspects. With three months' time and experience completed, both you and the firm will have a much better idea of how best to maximize your time and energy. I have found that most misunderstandings about workload in a new role can get worked out smoothly within three months on the job, provided there is regular and honest communication up and down the pipeline. So do not worry too much about initial workload issues.

At the same time, there are some *cultural* giants that can be harder to handle.

Joe Robles was drafted into the army during the Vietnam War, eventually working his way up to the rank of major general—a remarkable ascent for a young man of his time. He eventually retired from the military and became the president and CEO of USAA, one of the largest banking and insurance companies in the United States. But as a young man, he learned the importance of studying his new setting and adapting quickly.

He had served for a time in Vietnam when the army offered to send him back to the States to get his college degree before completing his military service. He enrolled at a college near his home and proudly showed up in uniform. What he did not know was that while he had been in Vietnam, a whole cultural phenomenon of protesting the war had broken out. His first day on campus was jarring as he was quite literally hit by culture shock: two female students threw paint-filled balloons at him, ruining his polished and starched uniform. He did not know that the National Guard had just shot and killed four protesting students on his campus, Kent State University. We have to consider how our presence will be perceived in our new setting and do our best to find ways to make friends early on. We need not be scared off by difficult challenges but rather prepared to overcome as we encounter them.

## THE PERILS OF PRESUMPTION

On December 11, 1998, NASA launched the Mars Climate Orbiter. The Orbiter was part of a program in the 1990s and early 2000s created to learn more about the surface and climate of Mars, our nearby planetary neighbor. Specifically, the Mars Climate Orbiter carried instruments designed to detect water, monitor weather patterns, look for evidence of past climate change, and make a number of other observations.[5] It was a highly advanced piece of technology that cost $327 million. The data it gathered would open new doors for planetary science. But instead of delivering on its great promise, the Orbiter exploded. It was launched and sent on its nine-month journey to the red planet with no problem whatsoever. But as soon as it arrived in Martian orbit, radio contact was lost—permanently.

In the weeks after the failed mission, NASA scientists realized what had gone wrong. The Orbiter had been a sophisticated piece of technology, programmed with software copied in triplicate to avoid any chances of a miscalculation or error. Much like the *Titanic,* it was designed to be foolproof, composed of dozens of systems and software programs acting in tandem. All these components coordinated perfectly, except one. NASA had purchased a certain piece of software from a US aerospace company. This would not have been a problem except that NASA used the metric system for all its instruments and software, whereas this firm's technology did not. Measurements of acceleration that NASA's instruments were reading as newtons had been provided instead as pound force-seconds. The discrepancy between the two units is roughly 4.5 to 1. The ensuing miscalculation forced the Orbiter to fly much closer to Mars than it should have, and so this miracle of space engineering ended up meeting its untimely demise in the planet's upper atmosphere.[6] The great loss had been caused by a very human error: a failure to check. The scientists at NASA had designed the Orbiter to be based on the metric system, and they *presumed* that all subcomponents would be as well.

When faced with transitions, we too often similarly presume that things in our new spaces will be like they were in our old ones—or at least we presume that we will be able to figure it out in the moment. Both are mistakes of hubris, and they can be avoided if we are willing to admit our limitations and those of the world around us. This is part of how we land well.

Looking ahead is invaluable, but of course it is not infallible. Despite our natural desire to understand everything before we move forward, there is only so much we can learn before we get there. There is an old romantic image in Shakespeare's *Henry V*. Outnumbered and surrounded in France, King Henry puts on a disguise to move about his camp the night before battle, seeking to find what his men really think of him. He learns more than he had hoped as he hears some men doubt his courage and motive. This knowledge helps him change some of his plans before the battle. Henry survives, in part, because of his reconnaissance. Now knowing what his men think of him, he rallies them with one of the most famous soliloquies in all of Shakespeare's corpus, urging "we happy few, we band of brothers" to join in battle on Saint Crispin's Day.[7]

Poetry aside, there are always things we cannot anticipate and surprises that occur in new places, like a flood that comes on suddenly, or a balloon filled with paint. Reality has no qualms about tempering our expectations. But that is why we have to be grounded in our convictions and use the "settled" times of our lives to develop virtue through daily practices. In so doing, we can make peace with ourselves and the people we are becoming, for this will matter even more as we transition to new places.

> Looking ahead is invaluable, but of course it is not infallible.

## IMPRESSION + IMPRESSION + IMPRESSION = REPUTATION

When the New England Patriots picked up Jonas Gray as a new running back, he knew he needed to perform. He had been on the roster for two NFL teams before then but due to injuries had not seen any action on the field. It was critically important that he make a good first impression on the team, and he succeeded. In his first major debut as a professional running back, he rushed for over two hundred yards and carried the ball thirty-eight times for four touchdowns. He was the first player in modern football to score four touchdowns in a game that he entered with no career points. He could not have performed better, *and* he made that week's cover of *Sports Illustrated*. The Patriots were elated, and Gray's projected career trajectory was nothing but up and to the right.

However, that's not how it played out. It was not an old injury that cut him down in his prime; it was a low battery. The next week, Gray forgot to charge his phone the night before practice. It ran out of power and didn't wake him up in time. The coach of the Patriots, Bill Belichick, is an accomplished hardliner with a zero-tolerance policy for tardiness. Gray was late, so Gray was not allowed to practice, and to Belichick, those who do not practice do not play in the next game.

That was the beginning of the end for the running back. For the entire rest of the season, he only posted ninety-one yards as the coach gave deference to other players. The Patriots would go on to win the Super Bowl that year, but without Gray's help—not even one scrimmage. By the start of the next season, he had been cut from the team.

It's unlikely that you will have a boss as strict as Belichick. But that's NFL football for you, and Belichick's record speaks for itself. Keep this story in the back of your mind, though, as a cautionary tale. First impressions matter; they set you up for success. But true success requires a stellar *reputation*, which is composed of all your impressions strung together. Think of your reputation as a pie chart with two fields, one for positive impressions and one for negative ones. If your first impression is great, then your pie chart is one green-filled circle. But a negative second impression now creates a half-and-half green-and-red circle. That's a major change. A good third and fourth impression will help, now creating a circle that's only one-quarter red. But that's still a lot of area. The point is that the earlier on in the process, the more your impressions matter to your overall reputation. Three hundred impressions later, your reputation is pretty well set, because each additional data point is only going to change the overall pie chart an infinitesimal amount.

So what's the takeaway here? Keep that circle green. When something is important, really important, don't leave anything to chance. If you're "new to the game," like Gray, realize that *your habits aren't set yet for optimal performance.* Your "mental notes" about your new responsibilities are likely to be deleted by your short-term memory. If you have to get up early for work, ask a friend to remind you to set your alarm. Or set two alarms—one across the room. In that vein, overprepare for your first meeting; you'll get the hang of how much you actually need to prepare later. For another example, if your professor says she doesn't take late papers, that probably means that she doesn't take late papers! Set an alert on your phone to remind you five hours before a paper is due.

In the case of a transition that you're being *forced* to make, like moving from a flooded home or recovering from a severe injury, sometimes the impressions you make are on yourself. Don't miss a doctor's appointment. Do your physical therapy exercises without fail. Keep up self-care. Accept help with gratitude. Continually pray and practice God's love toward others. This way you're making it clear to yourself that you are valuable and worth keeping around and investing in. Our souls really do listen to what we tell them.

The journey of building a reputation for yourself is a long and unfinishable one, but it is simply a fact that the early weeks and months matter for its overall trajectory. The relationships you have with others in your space are nothing more or less than the sum of your interactions with them, and as long as you are interacting you are impressing (or failing to). Everyone knows that you're on your best game with your first impression. It's the second and following ones where people expect to find out what you're *really* like.

## BUILDING THE CULTURE

As a guest in the early days of your transition, it's important to understand the concept of *culture* and to grasp its implications in your new space. Eventually, you will become one of the builders of this culture. Culture, simply put, is the sum of all the behaviors, practices, and norms that are maintained by people in a community. If your supervisor makes a habit of taking the office out to lunch, that is part of your workplace culture. If your colleagues routinely show up five minutes late for meetings, that's workplace culture too. Behaviors like these are not merely independent phenomena; when repeated by members of the community with authority, they become normative.

Culture can be described as meaning making. Authors Andy Crouch and Ken Myers have rightly defined culture as what we *make* of the world—in both senses of that term.[8] It is what we produce through our life works (things such as business deals, new electronic devices, healthier patients, and stronger communities) *and* the interpretive lens that we bring to everything around us.

There are many ways you can see evidence of culture in your new space. It is not only about rules and policies but also unspoken expectations. It is made evident in the way we organize work and workflows, in the various roles that people occupy, and in the ways that we recognize and reward one another. These ideas go back to the writings of Max Weber, the pioneering German thinker of the early twentieth century who predicted that society would come to be dominated by large institutions.[9] As we transition from one place to another, it is vital to study and embrace the organizational culture of our new home.

Sometimes the regular, everyday culture of a space is difficult to "hear" above the sounds of all the messages the governors of the culture want to communicate to you. Your boss, your peers, your new university, even your new in-laws want to make a good impression on you. They want to share two things with you: things *you* want to hear, and things *they* want you to hear. The former is all about the message that this is a good space to be in. The latter is about how you're expected to behave in this new space. And they will send these messages both overtly and subtly.

When high school students tour a college campus, the guides take them through the nicest residence halls. The food they serve is always the best a school can offer. They make sure they meet with the best and brightest current students and professors. This is no accident. It is the same with a new job at a new company. No employee orientation features a video of the CEO recounting all the lawsuits from last year or talking about the liquidity challenges the company is facing in Q4. That is not what they want to communicate to new hires. Instead, new and potential employees hear about the organization's amenities, opportunities, and legacy. When an establishment presents you with the best and brightest, they are hoping to communicate that these superlatives are actually the norm. It's not deception in the sinister sense. It's how a business, school, or even family hopes to improve itself. If they show the best they have to offer, and a person identifies with that and is drawn to it, then theoretically the exemplary case can one day become the average as standards rise.

Culture can't help but communicate itself, sometimes indirectly. I have been on a college tour where the tour guide answered a student's question by saying, "Well, you won't really have time for friends, because you'll be studying too hard." That answer communicated a lot more about the school than the guide probably realized. It said, *"Our culture is one where academic performance is everything. If you don't share this priority, you won't fit in here."* There are some schools, on the other hand, that market themselves (or allow themselves to be marketed) as "party schools." This says, *"Our culture values a good time and won't ask too much of you academically."* Both extremes communicate expectations for your behavior once you have crossed the threshold onto campus.

So pay attention to the culture of a new space, and not just at the surface level. In your first few days and weeks into a transition, notice the kinds of norms and cultural artifacts you are exposed to. What are the awards on the wall? Whose stories are told at the break table? What icons are revered, and whose faults are ignored? For better or worse, these are norms to which you will be expected to conform.

It may be that in the course of time, you, like Gail McGovern, get the chance to change some of the institutional expectations. But that is not what first days are for. First days are for learning the culture of your new space while you are still a guest. First days are for first impressions. And first impressions are the springboards for second and third impressions, which, if you work hard enough, might just change you and your new space for the better as you land well.

# 5

# THE DEADBOLT

## EARNING THE KEY THROUGH TRUST

*Do not conform to the pattern of this world,*
*but be transformed by the renewing of your mind.*
*Then you will be able to test and approve what*
*God's will is—his good, pleasing and perfect will.*

ROMANS 12:2

RICHARD HAD MADE ALL the wrong decisions in life. At the age of eighteen, he was convicted of murder and sentenced to twenty-two years in prison. On his release at age forty, he had never held a job. He had never even driven a car. He enrolled in a program that helps ex-convicts land jobs to reduce recidivism. Richard took a job as an exterminator. It was not a glorious position, but it was something. In a later interview, he was asked if he was happy. Richard responded simply by showing a text on his phone he had received from his boss: "Emergency bed-bug job East 65th Street. I need you now." That was Richard's answer to the question about happiness: "It says *I need you now*. Nobody had ever said that to me in my whole life."[1]

Being needed means that you have a role, an important purpose, and that people are relying on you, confident that you can and will carry it out. Being needed means, simply put, that you belong. Though your background experiences are likely remarkably different from Richard's, we are all much the same in this: true happiness and satisfaction in life come from belonging.

> **True happiness and satisfaction in life come from belonging.**

As you enter the *integration* phase of transition, you will develop deeper connections with others in the new space, and you will find more people you can trust even as they find you trustworthy. Simple practices like keeping a journal can remind you of ways that God is moving as you become more fully integrated into the new place. You'll want to develop regular practices to meet people, forcing yourself to leave your desk or office and meet others, and going out of your way to get to know the new place and its unique history and culture. In the process, you'll develop a deeper appreciation for this place where God has led you and find ways to become invaluable to others.

## BELONGING AND VULNERABILITY

At the start of a transition the door before us is open and we focus on crossing the threshold. Toward the end of a successful transition, however, we will begin to see the door closing behind us. All doors have to be able to close—and many to lock—or else they would never be useful for security. Something has to keep out the riffraff, after all. As you transition from one space to another, it will be up to you to take on the identity of the limited number of people who *belong* behind this locked door. It will be up to you to earn your key.

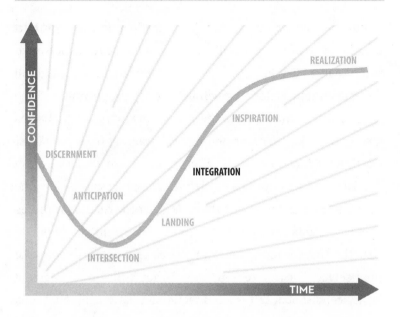

Full adoption into membership and belonging in your new space is neither discrete nor instantaneous. It is a process. You may get the keys to your new home or your ID badge for school or work on your first day there, but membership rightly understood is a process of becoming both *trustworthy to* and *trusting of* the institution and the people in it. And family transitions—such as getting married or becoming a parent—are fundamentally about becoming trustworthy and trusting the other. Indeed, development of this bidirectional trust is fundamental to success in the transition to our new lives because trust is the gateway to meaningful contribution. This is how you discover and embody God's purpose for your new place in life.

> Membership rightly understood is a process of becoming both *trustworthy to* and *trusting of* the institution and the people in it

But trust requires vulnerability. It is an openness to being hurt when that trust is breached, and it is a chance to be bolstered when that trust is kept. The pace of your transition toward full and meaningful belonging will be directly proportional to the speed at which the others in the space come to trust you. What is more, you will never stop adding or detracting from your trustworthiness; it is a perpetual system of credits to which we make deposits and withdrawals over time. The process is a slow one because trust is a precious thing. Misplaced trust, be it professional, personal, romantic, or of any other kind can be so destructive that the reputation for these sorts of betrayals speak for themselves. For this reason, trust is not built on niceties but rather consistencies. It is a bidirectional relationship built on a shared history over a period of time.

Social belonging, then, is the culmination of long and consistent bidirectional reliability. It is long in that it takes time to build up. The pain of breaches of trust and of the vulnerability required for relationships of trust make trust building a slow process. The epidemic of divorce in our culture is just one contributing factor these days to the reluctance of young people to trust— as kids see their own parents or others diminish trust in their families—and if one does not trust others, that person is less likely to become trustworthy to others. Talking a big game about trust is a far cry from showing yourself strong in it. Ultimately, the most trustworthy people need not persuade others about it. If someone says, "No, this time *I promise*," that is an indication of a reputation tarnished by distrust. Whether forming new relationships at college, in your new neighborhood, in your new office, with a new spouse and in-laws, or even with your child as a new parent (babies learn to trust when they are fed, comforted, and responded to), the people in your new space will be watching to learn whether or not they can trust you with information, questions, projects, and secrets. People who make themselves untrustworthy through action or inaction will find it difficult to become an insider or to ever truly belong.

## TRUST IN THEORY AND PRACTICE

Trustworthiness is a notoriously difficult virtue to nail down. Its scope ranges from the obvious—doing what we said we were going to do—to the nebulous (but ever-present) social "stickiness" that holds relationships and communities together. It's vaguely related to loyalty, but it's more of a character trait than a choice. Although trust is a slippery concept to define, we recognize it when we see it, and when it is lacking we do not function optimally.

The most basic instinct all animals share is the drive to survive. Animals have developed different strategies to do this and in doing so have produced the variety of life we see today. For us "moral, believing animals," as sociologist Chris Smith puts it,[2] otherwise known as humans, our competitive advantage is not wings, venom, or fangs, but cooperation. In fact, our ability to engage in symbolic communication (language) for the sake of cooperation is one of our most defining features as a species.[3] This cooperation is the reason we can develop communities, and communities thrive on trust. In everyday life it's easy for us to assess without thinking whether we trust someone or not, or whether we feel safe in a situation or not. So, although trust is difficult to define, evaluations of trustworthiness are second nature to us.

Furthermore, research suggests there is a complex but positively correlated relationship between levels of trust in a community and levels of health and wellbeing. A study of over twenty thousand Americans found that after controlling for income and education, individuals who lived in high-trust communities (where the respondents felt they could trust their neighbors) were more likely to report multiple indicators of health and wellbeing than were those who did not.[4] However, this was only true for those people who were themselves highly trusted by others. This means that people in communities with high levels of social trust can benefit greatly but only if they themselves engender trust. So trust only works when it goes both ways. To want to be trusted by others and yet to trust no one—or the other way around—is pathological.

Trust is even more powerful than many of us realize. In low-income communities, it can work *against* certain social forces that keep people impoverished. It was once thought that people remain poor because of some individual deficiency (such as laziness or stupidity). More recently we have come to understand that the dominant factors are systemic rather than personal. One of the chief contributing factors of cyclical poverty is what social scientists refer to as "poverty-induced myopic decision-making." In short, poverty affects people in such a way that they become less able to make decisions with long-term payoffs that would benefit them and more likely to make a worse decision that looks attractive in the short term (for instance, spending money on something they want now rather than saving for something better in the future, or taking a lower-paying job now rather than pursuing education for a higher-paying job later). Making the choice for a higher long-term payout requires *trust* in a *system*. Many people stuck in a cycle of poverty have learned not to trust the systems around them for one reason or another.

A study conducted in Bangladesh by researchers at Stanford University found that over time people in low-income communities who developed communal trust were less likely to make these characteristically myopic decisions. Specifically, the researchers found that increased levels of trust were able to decrease the "temporal discounting" that in many cases makes long-term planning difficult.[5]

Studies like these are a reminder that trust is part and parcel of the human condition. If you yourself are not struggling with systemic myopic decision-making, you are blessed. You have grown up in a situation where you have been able to trust the people and systems around you.

Dr. Paul Zak's pioneering work on neuroscience and economic life demonstrates why trust is so vital to new settings, especially in the workplace. He notes, "Experiments around the world have shown that humans are naturally inclined to trust others—but don't always."[6] As it turns out, neurochemicals make a huge difference in our likelihood to trust another person and in our becoming trustworthy to others. The release of a hormone called oxytocin into the bloodstream by the pituitary gland increases a person's empathy and greatly reduces that person's fear of trusting another person. In fact, oxytocin has been called the friendship hormone; it serves as a neurotransmitter to reinforce attachment between people, starting as early as the bond between a mother and her infant. It helps kids get along on the playground and facilitates the process of falling in love with a future spouse.

From research sites in Papua, New Guinea, to corporate America, Zak and colleagues found that greater degrees of oxytocin create a more trusting social milieu in which to live and work. But more than just connecting, oxytocin enables us to *categorize* people, places, and things as in-group (which we seek out and are drawn toward) and out-group (which we avoid and repel). In other words, you begin to associate with certain people and dissociate with others at least in part because of the neurochemical's release into the body. This is why early forms of connection and bonding with others in your new environment will play such a formative role in your sense of belonging over the long haul. Without conscious thought, your experiences become powerful frames of thinking that reinforce your self-understandings with each subsequent interaction. Of course, what is happening in your body is happening to others as well. You want their brains to associate you as a member of their group, someone with whom they belong and to whom they grant confidence and faith.

As Zak found, "When people care about one another, they perform better, because they don't want to let their teammates down." High-trust environments care about the whole person, not simply one dimension, so it is worthwhile for you to take an interest in your colleagues' family, hobbies, and life story as you come to learn about them. Ask questions to get to know them better. Invite them and their family to your home for a weekend barbeque. Connect over shared experiences. (The sharing of intense, life-altering experiences, such as adopting a child or battling cancer, have a profound way of creating a sense of solidarity and camaraderie.) In the process, you may not only develop a new friendship but you will also increase the odds that your new work team will be a winning one.

Indeed, those who work in high-trust environments report enjoying their jobs 60 percent more, indicate they are 70 percent more aligned with their company's purpose, and feel 66 percent closer to their colleagues than do workers in environments that aren't perceived as high trust. And the benefits are monetary too. On average, employees earn 17 percent more at companies in the highest quartile of trust compared to the lowest quartile, according to Zak's research.

Surprisingly, the high-trust environments discovered by Zak were not typically places with lax expectations and easy-to-follow procedures. They were actually places with a higher than average amount of workplace stress, coupled with flexibility in how to respond. People in these workplaces were working and thinking harder than most, but they were also trusting harder. This combination of freedom in a framework of frenzy actually promotes the release of oxytocin and another neurochemical, adrenocorticotropin. Their combined release is correlated with tighter interpersonal bonds between people and greater individual focus.

The ideal level of "challenge" stress is achieved, then, with goals that stretch beyond individual capabilities and necessitate that people work together to share resources, responsibilities, or both. This is the ideal context in which to work; the net result is a much more fulfilling job and workplace. A study by Citigroup and LinkedIn found that nearly half of employees would forego a 20 percent raise in favor of greater control over how they work. So as the newcomer, be on the lookout for offices or teams that get a lot done. That's where you want to end up. Find ways to become a contributor to that group's collective work, even if it requires volunteering after hours. Finding a place of high trust and generous freedom will make a huge difference in your long-term satisfaction and professional contribution.

## TELL THE TRUTH BY YOUR ACTIONS

Unlike some of his contemporaries, Aristotle conceptualized virtue not as an appeal to some objective and celestial standard of perfection but rather as something gained through habit and practice. The virtuous person, therefore, was not the one who *knew* the most about virtue but the one who *practiced* it the most. In *The Speed of Trust,* Steven Covey declares, "We judge ourselves by our intentions and others by their behavior. This is why . . . one of the fastest ways to restore trust is to make and keep commitments—even very small commitments—to ourselves and to others."[7] Those around you do not hear your inner monologue or understand the moral calculus you might have undertaken before you took a particular action. They merely see what you did, and they infer your motives from whatever seemed to happen plus what they already know about you. This seemingly simple truth illuminates exactly why trust can be so elusive—especially in new settings and even for trustworthy people. So you have to be proactive. Just as a student's performance on the piano improves with regular practice, so also does your ability to display trustworthiness through your actions.

Bernard Arnault is the wealthiest man in the fashion world and has at times been the richest man on the planet. He is the chairman and chief executive of Louis Vuitton Moët Hennessy (LVMH), which leads the world in sales of many high-end luxury goods, from wine to jewelry to clothing. LVMH's first non-French acquisition was a company called Duty Free Shops (the ones you see in airports), which was at the time being run by my friend Mike Ullman. After acquiring the company, Arnault kept Ullman on as the head of Duty Free Shops and slowly built up a strong relationship with him.

Mike told me about a conversation he and Arnault had one afternoon in which Arnault surprisingly asked him to come to Paris and help run the entirety of the LVMH empire. Mike responded with obvious shock, reminding the multibillionaire that he did not speak French and did not particularly want to move to Paris. Mike asked him, "Why do you want me?" Arnault's answer was sincere: "I have so many people reporting to me . . . and I really need someone who is going to be a truth teller."

A few things from this story stand out. I can personally attest to Mike Ullman's highly trustworthy character. He served as Gordon College's vice chair of the board for some years, and we worked closely together that whole time. So it did not surprise me to learn that Arnault found him to be honest, direct, and trustworthy. What did surprise me is that one of the wealthiest people on the planet was just looking for an honest man to be his second-in-command. He was not looking for an aggressive leader or financial mastermind (though Mike certainly has tremendous business acumen). What he needed was someone who would tell him the truth.

Honesty and trustworthiness are rarer than you might expect at the peaks of power and influence. It is a strange paradox when you think about it. One of the very first things we teach children is the value of honesty. We tell countless stories and fables to ingrain the virtue. However, its apparent rarity in the upper echelons of society is stern warning that it too often gets lost on the way up. What are some of the best safeguards against this moral decay?

First, don't just tell the truth; tell the truth early. Imagine that your practice of the virtue is like making deposits at the bank of trustworthiness. There must be a positive balance in order for later withdrawals to work. If you wait until you are hired to tell your boss that you need to take off a few days in your second week to attend a cousin's wedding, you are already starting in the red for that relationship (you should have said something about that before you signed on).

The fact is that one day you will find yourself at your desk in the wee hours experiencing that sad realization that you just will not meet the deadline. When you send that email asking for an extension, your professor or boss is going to think back on your track record. Up until this point, have you been turning in your best work on time or even ahead of time? Is this a rare request coming from you? Have you kept in touch about your progress so that this isn't a total surprise? There is often grace for those with steady track records and reputations for consistent trustworthiness. A good supervisor will understand and be accommodating for those rare extenuating circumstances.

That said, it is a good idea when taking on responsibilities to make it your motto to underpromise and overdeliver. Be honest about the deadlines you can meet and your own limitations. Build in some margin for unexpected problems (if they never arise, then you'll be able to finish early). Then shoot to exceed the standard.

When your supervisor gives you a project and says, "Let's circle back in a week," he or she should never have to do the circling back. Promptly deliver updates on projects as they are completed and be forthcoming when unforeseen difficulties arise. New employees often have a tendency of underreporting and under-updating their supervisors for fear of seeming overly eager or naïve. But I have seen very few supervisors who complain about too much transparency from their direct reports. When in doubt, update.

If the update is good and you share it, that is an opportunity to highlight your work. If the update is bad, that is a chance to demonstrate transparency and ask for help. If the update is good and you do not share it, that is a missed opportunity and an open invitation for others to presume negative things. The worst case is when the update is bad and you choose not to share it. Not only will you later suffer the consequences of whatever the failure was, but you'll be considered underhanded for keeping it to yourself. Others will think, *"What else is this person hiding?"*

Mike Ullman's story is a prime example of the fact that long-standing relationships marked by honesty engender trust. Whether your boss is Bernard Arnault or your professor in class, the same principles apply: membership begins with trustworthiness, and trustworthiness begins with honesty. It is tempting to think you can get away with minor misrepresentations here and there, but these things often have ways of catching up with us. For every person who successfully builds a good relationship and reputation for trustworthiness, there are those who make the wrong choices.

## RESIST RUTHLESSNESS

Maurice "Hank" Greenberg was a longtime legendary chairman and CEO of the American International Group (AIG). He led the company for forty-seven years, and under his watch it became the world's largest insurer, valued at almost half a trillion dollars. He had done as well as anyone in the private sector ever could, but he pushed the ethical boundaries throughout his career, firing two of his own sons from the firm and developing a reputation as a ferocious executive. In my interview with him, he talked about how, as a young man, he forced his way into an executive's office at a company where he wanted to work, demanding a job. Surprisingly, he got it. Many observers predicted that this kind of behavior at age twenty-five would eventually catch up with him, yet he almost retired unscathed. But a fraud case nearly destroyed AIG in the mid-2000s.

Under Greenberg's watch, AIG misrepresented accounting figures in their quest to increase their quarterly profit margins after some bad investments. His decision to win at whatever cost, first cultivated at the start of his career, had manifested itself in corporate dishonesty. AIG entered a death spiral during the housing crisis of the Great Recession and was designated "too big to fail" by the federal government. They were ultimately given an $85 billion loan in 2008, but Ben Bernanke, chairman of the Federal Reserve, said that nothing made him angrier during the financial crisis than the conduct of AIG. At age seventy-nine, Greenberg was finally forcibly removed from the empire he had built. To this day, he is seen as a tragic figure whose actions contributed greatly to the financial crisis of 2007–2008. He is a prime example of how much dishonesty can undo good and how much potential good it can poison. He demonstrates, also, that unlike certain firms and companies, individuals are *never* too big to fail.

I am sure that to Greenberg, AIG's misconduct seemed innocent enough. He probably thought it did not hurt anyone, and if it did, it was only the shareholders, and if it *did* hurt the shareholders, it was only temporary. This is the kind of rationalizing self-justification we can find ourselves engaging in if we do not practice the virtues necessary for becoming good members of communities and institutions. Greenberg might have appeared to others as overconfident, but the reality is that it takes a deep insecurity to manifest such bald-faced duplicity.

Maybe one day you will be in Greenberg's position, making decisions that affect tens of thousands of people. Or maybe you won't. Either way, you must decide now, if you haven't already, how far you are willing to go to reach the goals you believe you must achieve. Will you be a truth teller, or someone who only tells the parts that make you look good? Or worse, someone who will say and do whatever it takes to get what you want? That's called ruthlessness, and it's led many an unprincipled person in power to justify deceit—and even cruelty.

Get a head start now on the temptations coming your way by practicing reliability rather than ruthlessness. If your new roommate in college asks for a ride to the airport, say yes if it's in your power. Ruthlessness says that your roommate is an adult and should be able to figure it out himself; you've got better things to do with your time. Reliability says that if someone needs something and it is reasonably in your power to help, you do so. Even more critically, if you say you will do something, do it! (Nothing sours a new relationship faster than a last-minute cancellation and a scramble for an Uber at 6:00 a.m.) If your friend tells you something in confidence, keep that confidence. If your Q3 earnings are embarrassing, report them accurately anyway.

Trustworthiness and reliability require consistent and predictable actions every time, not merely when convenient. Deliver quality results and make good on your promises long enough, and you will transition in the eyes of your peers and supervisors from "the new guy" to a full-fledged member of the team.

> Trustworthiness and reliability require consistent and predictable actions every time, not merely when convenient.

## EARN YOUR KEY

A closed door is a better deterrent than nothing, but only a locked door can really keep safe what is behind it. Keys to such doors provide individuals with authority to open and close the space as they see fit, and in doing so influence the space itself. Sometimes we earn the confidence and trust of others by being willing to speak up even when it's unpopular or upsetting.

Rachael Denhollander was a homeschooler and gymnast from Kalamazoo, Michigan. She coached gymnastics at a local club and became a lawyer in her early twenties. Within a decade, she would become a worldwide role model for publicly accusing USA gymnastics doctor Larry Nassar of sexual abuse. Before she was heralded worldwide for her courage and inspirational leadership, though, she faced the harsh reality of pushing against the institutional inertia at Michigan State University and the de facto assumption that accusers are rarely right, especially when the accused is a recognized and seasoned professional.

Denhollander led the charge against Nassar and spoke as an attorney herself in his trial. Two hundred women testified against him, and he eventually pled guilty and is now serving four hundred years of jail time. It seems unfathomable today that such crimes could go on for so many decades without justice. But this is the sticky reality about culture: whether it's good or bad, culture is difficult to change. It often takes a pioneer like Denhollander to fight to change a culture for the better. Since the Nassar trial, she has dedicated her time to abuse education and advocacy, drawing on her Christian faith to help women challenge cultures of abuse toward building a more just society. When she confronted Nassar face-to-face in the courtroom, she quoted the Bible and C. S. Lewis in making her case.

This power of culture making and unmaking is a part of nearly all transitions. You will not learn everything about a space on day one, and you will not be able to change much about it either, at least not early on. But as grow into your new space, be attentive not only to the good but also the bad, and be prepared to use your cultural influence to make your new place better for all.

## THE INTEGRATED PRACTICE UNIT

When trust flourishes among people and across groups, organizations and communities dramatically improve and thrive. Angela Duckworth is a psychologist at the University of Pennsylvania and the world's leading expert on *grit*. She defines *grit* as the passion and perseverance required to achieve long-term goals.[8] Her work on the subject has been remarkably influential in everything from business to the US military to education. Writing on effective workplaces, she would seem to agree with the findings of Zak discussed earlier: The "optimal environment will be both demanding and supportive. People will be asked to meet high expectations, which will be clearly defined and feasible though challenging. But they'll also be offered the psychological safety and trust."[9]

The best settings are those that have high expectations, room to fail, and trust that flows in both directions. In her work, Duckworth makes reference to a type of organizational structure particular to the medical industry as a gold standard for cooperation, membership, and success. It is called the "integrated practice unit" (IPU). This unit is a group of multidisciplinary doctors, nurses, and staff who, when working in tandem, provide the full cycle of treatment and service to a patient in need. She writes that two of the IPU's defining features are "shared purpose" and "mutual trust."[10] These units succeed so well because there is a continuous sense of need and belonging, as well as mutual trust shared among members. Everyone in the unit needs everyone else, and together they can provide exactly what the patient needs 100 percent of the time. Although healthcare is unique in some ways, the integrated practice unit is, at its core, a problem-solving team. And every career (and by extension every office) on the planet exists to solve a problem. Therefore, the IPU is a model with lessons for every workplace.

Teams with shared goals and bidirectional trust are going to be able to do more than individuals or trustless teams could ever hope to accomplish. That's why a successful transition is nothing less than effectively establishing yourself as someone who belongs on the team—someone whom somebody else needs and trusts. Never forget about Richard, who after his release from prison, finally found happiness. But he had to transition to that space from a difficult position: that of an ex-con. The difficulty of transition is always in that liminal space between spaces, where the new trust and membership you need in order to succeed is there potentially but not yet actually.

Richard was not happy because he got to kill bedbugs. He was not happy because he was good at it. He flourished because he was *needed*. And he was needed because his boss trusted him. And trust—more than talent, temperament, or even tenacity—is the key to your long-term success.

# 6

# THE HINGE

## THE VIRTUE OF AFFIXED FLEXIBILITY

*A reed before the wind lives on, while mighty oaks do fall.*

GEOFFREY CHAUCER

MORE THAN THE THRESHOLD or the lock, the humble hinge is the most important part of the door. You probably never interact with the hinges on your doors—unless it is to quiet their squeaking with some WD-40 every so often. But without a hinge, the door would be merely an unwieldy slab propped against a gap in the wall. The hinge makes the door useable but also fixes it into its frame. So it both enables and limits; a well-hinged door is both free and fixed.

Like a hinge, a "hinge moment" changes everything. It entails an abrupt turn from one thing to another, but it also means new possibilities—new avenues to new spaces. These are the moments when we are tested, when we either make the most of our transitions or we waste them. Or worse, we let them waste us. When we aren't properly prepared for our hinge moments, we can panic and make choices we regret later and maybe for the rest of our lives. But if we have robust, reliable hinges, we can make the choices and take the actions that lead to successful transitions.

When we aren't properly prepared for our hinge moments, we can panic and make choices we regret later.

Once you move beyond the low point of the intersection stage of transition, the landing and integration phases provide opportunities for your confidence to grow and your comfort level to increase. And now you reach the *inspiration* stage of transition. This is the point when you become a resource for others, particularly those experiencing earlier phases of their own personal transitions (perhaps marrying into your family, enrolling at your school, or starting a job at your firm). During the inspiration phase, you begin to make sense and find meaning behind the changes you've experienced—even tough ones like losing a loved one or being

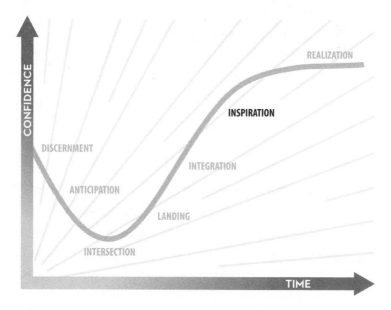

laid off. In so doing, your confidence level continues to rise, and you begin to see yourself flourishing—at least in part—thanks to the transition that has occurred.

## HINGE VIRTUES

Pivoting well requires firm and unshakeable hinges in your life. These are the constants that keep you steady and stable when you have to make changes. Like literal door hinges, they provide freedom within a framework. Long before you or I worried about which college or job to apply to, philosophers and the fathers of the faith were hard at work naming these life hinges. They called them the cardinal virtues.

The word *cardinal* is from a Latin term referring to the hinge of a door. The idea was that these virtues were the necessary hinges on which we should hang our lives. The four virtues of prudence, fortitude, temperance, and justice have been a mainstay of both sacred and secular Western ethical thought for thousands of years. They were touted by Plato and by Roman politicians such as Cicero and Marcus Aurelius. Ambrose, the bishop of Milan and pastor to Augustine, was the first to attach the word *cardinal* to a list of virtues, and it has been part of the church's teaching for faithful disciples ever since.

## PRUDENCE: THE CHARIOTEER

The first of the cardinal virtues is prudence, or applied wisdom. In the original Latin expression, the word had the sense of being able to see ahead, to make decisions *now* based on *what is likely to be.* Cicero saw the prudent person as one who knew how to weigh the consequences of words and actions before speaking or doing.

Thomas Aquinas, perhaps the greatest theologian of the Middle Ages, was the premier synthesizer of Christian and Aristotelian thought. He was the first to call wisdom the "charioteer of the virtues." In this sense, wisdom is the virtue that holds the reins for all others. You, like a horse, may be strong, healthy, and ready to run, but that does you little good if wisdom does not hold the reins of your life. Wisdom, then, must not be just understanding; it needs to be understanding applied in action—*prudence.* No matter which way transitions or possible transitions may try to pull you, this is the first and most important hinge to keep fast.

While researching great leaders, two things I was most interested in learning were what sources of wisdom they drew on when facing difficult choices and how they applied prudence (or failed to do so). Pierre Omidyar, the founder of eBay who led the company out of his garage into a multibillion-dollar IPO, told me that crucial to big decision-making for him was "going back to the core values of what it is that I'm really trying to do." Like the Romans, he thought hard about what *will be* from observing what *is*: "Will this decision be consistent with that, or will it help accelerate and support those values? Or will it work against it or make it more difficult for us to live by those values?"

> You, like a horse, may be strong, healthy, and ready to run, but that does you little good if wisdom does not hold the reins of your life.

Here is a double lesson: Yes, Omidyar used wisdom when he reflected on the values (read, *hinges*) on which his company had been established. But this wisdom needed prudence in order to make organization-altering decisions such as whether to accept this or that offer to buy his company. Omidyar has been so successful partly by being flexible and willing to take calculated risks. But he also always retains the values that have been the foundation on which he has built his enterprises.

We are people, of course, and not organizations, but the application is the same. We also have "core values," founding principles to our lives. Identifying and regularly returning to our hinges (and keeping wisdom and prudence among them) is the first step toward establishing and maintaining good hinges for life. Sometimes that comes from habits of reading widely and learning from others. Often, we develop prudence through experience and application of life's lessons learned in family, school, and work settings. But it also requires godly discernment and an authentic desire to use our wisdom to bless and serve others.

The writer of Ecclesiastes did not think very highly of traditional learning for its own sake: "the more knowledge, the more grief." And later he writes, "much study wearies the body" (Ecclesiastes 1:18; 12:12). Ecclesiastes suggests that the wise and the foolish reach the same end, which is not exactly an endorsement for acquiring wisdom. But on closer inspection, we see that the writer's comments are written to a particular context—namely, a life that is largely lived for oneself. In Ecclesiastes 2, for instance, there are no less than thirty references to the self (I, me, my, and myself), and the criticism of gaining wisdom or knowledge is primarily a critique about the end, the *telos,* to which the person is working. In essence, the teacher is raising an important issue to be considered in the quest for wisdom and its application—who or what are we orienting our lives around? Indeed, the teacher of Ecclesiastes is concerned about a mind fixed on itself, suggesting that a self-centered person (whether wise or foolish) strengthens power for the oppressors and denies comfort to the oppressed. Therefore, a fundamental question in the pursuit of wisdom is, *What's on my mind most of the time?* Put in other words: *For whom do I pray most often? In quiet, unguarded moments, what am I fantasizing about? What makes me most worried or anxious?*

A life of applied wisdom, the pathway of prudence, must be one intentionally focused on the *other*. That's really the only way to acquire and embody the virtue of prudence. It reminds me of a rabbinic story about one man's visit to hell. There he saw a long banquet table replete with sumptuous food and all the trimmings. The table was surrounded by starving people. The people were all holding awkwardly long spoons, too long to feed themselves. This made their situation all the more pitiful. The story continues as the man is next granted a visit to heaven. There he found a similar scene—the same table, the same food, and the same long spoons. The difference, however, was that in heaven they fed each other.

## BUILD FORTITUDE *BEFORE* YOU NEED IT

The second cardinal virtue is fortitude, or what we might today call courage. Socrates defined courage as "a man willing to remain at his post and to defend himself against the enemy without running away." There is something to be said for this kind of courage, but Christian tradition takes a slightly different approach. To the medieval Scholastics, courage meant "endurance," a willingness to stay at something. This is the steadfastness to which we are exhorted in so many passages of Scripture: Don't give up because God wins. Stand firm even when it seems the whole world bears down on you. It is to this end that Jesus promised his followers, "I have told you these things, so that in me you may have peace. In this world you will have trouble. But take heart! I have overcome the world" (John 16:33). God said to Joshua in the Old Testament, "Have I not commanded you? Be strong and courageous. Do not be afraid; do not be discouraged, for the Lord your God will be with you wherever you go" (Joshua 1:9). While we will hopefully feel up to displaying fortitude in the classroom by standing up for what we believe—and in our private lives, to resisting sin when the world is telling us that there's no such thing—"overcoming the world," as Jesus described, is surely another achievement altogether. This requires a fortitude that trusts that God is good *all* the time.

Several years ago, I met Phil Vischer. We sat down over coffee in his hometown of Wheaton, Illinois. In many ways, he has lived a storybook life. After all, Phil is the guy who created VeggieTales, one of the world's most successful children's video series. He had always admired Walt Disney, and as a young man he dreamed of building a media empire that could rival Disney but that was centered on a biblical, moral vision instead of just syrupy, entertaining stories.

Phil originally planned on using candy bars for his characters. But then his wife told him that mothers around the world would hate him for it, so he decided to give vegetables a try. For so many families, the characters have become household names. First, there's Bob the Tomato. He and his good friend, Larry the Cucumber, have presented many a moral tale in a warm, winsome manner. They often cover biblical stories, as in "Dave and the Giant Pickle," which retells the story of David and Goliath. But the creators of VeggieTales also drew inspiration from popular culture, infusing scenes and dialogues that retold parts of movies such as *Rocky* and *The Karate Kid.*

Between 1993 and 2003, VeggieTales was spectacularly successful. They sold over fifty million copies of various videos. They also launched product lines that included books, games, and toys. They even put together a full-length feature film titled *Jonah: A VeggieTales Movie.*

Phil talked to me about the evening of the movie's premier, which ironically was one of the worst nights of his life. As he and all his employees celebrated the film's premier with a red-carpet gala, Phil greeted the cheering crowd. However, he knew something that fans and employees would not learn about for another twelve hours: the company was about to declare bankruptcy, and most of the people celebrating that night would be losing their jobs the very next day.

Now there are lots of structural and financial reasons that led VeggieTales to this terrible demise, but for a moment consider Phil's predicament. He is a creative genius who did the impossible. He built a massive media empire whose products resonated with his Christian convictions and brought joy and happiness to millions of families around the world. In a matter of ten years, he took a story idea that began in his home office and made it into an international success. It was a lifelong dream come true. And then it all started to crumble. But by then, it was not simply Phil's dream. It was a dream that employed hundreds of people, affected thousands of families, and in many ways represented the respectability that Christians had worked hard to secure in the entertainment world.

Despite Phil's pleas and heartfelt prayers that God would intervene, for some reason, the Lord did not. Different media conglomerates took over parts of the VeggieTales empire, and because Phil was the voice of multiple characters they kept him on as a consultant. But now it was a different place, nowhere near the kind of organization it had been or that Phil had dreamed of since visiting Disneyland as a kid.

As we sat together in the coffee shop, I asked Phil how he kept going in the midst of this incredible loss. He started to talk about the Shunamite woman of 2 Kings 4. I was not familiar with the passage, but it's a remarkable story of surprising redemption. Elisha develops a friendship with an older couple and eventually prophesies that the woman will bear a son; despite her disbelief, she bears a child one year later. For a moment, everything is perfect in her life. But then the inexplicable happens. One morning the little boy goes to his father complaining about his head, and within hours he dies in his mother's arms. The Bible gives no indication of why this happened or how the elderly couple processed their grief, but we know it had to be heartbreaking.

As the Scriptures tell, the woman lays the boy's body in the guest bedroom she had constructed for Elisha, and then she sets out to find the prophet on Mount Carmel. She ends up persuading Elisha to return to her home, in hopes that he might be able to do something to revive her son. What follows is one of the most extraordinary accounts in the Old Testament. Elisha goes to the room and prays, eventually stretching out over the boy's body, eyes on eyes, hands on hands. At first the boy's body only becomes warm, but on a second attempt, he starts sneezing. In fact, he sneezes seven times. Eventually, the little boy rises, and the prophet reunites the son with his mother. This remarkable passage records one of just a handful of moments in Scripture when the dead are brought back to life. In this case it occurs, at least in part, because of the fortitude of the mother and the faithfulness of the prophet.

The story of the Shunamite woman and the tale of Phil Vischer remind us that God is the giver of good gifts. Sometimes those gifts are taken away. And in some situations, those gifts can be given back to us, as happened with the Shunamite's son. The Bible teaches that God can be moved to action by the prayers of the righteous. But we also have to realize that sometimes those prayers are not answered as we would like. That's the story of Phil Vischer and VeggieTales. He prayed, and the miracle didn't come. Why not?

Miracles occur as signs of a new creation. We believe that sometime in the future, God is going to make everything new. The book of Revelation speaks of a "new heaven and a new earth" (Revelation 21:1). When miracles do occur, they are moments of that new creation breaking into our world. That's why they captivate our attention; they make good on the promise God has given us to make all things new. They remind us that we serve and obey a God who is sovereign and can bring life out of death. They also remind us that ours is a God who will do what he says he will do. Throughout Scripture, the faithful are exhorted to remain faithful, to hold fast. This side of eternity, there is much that we do not understand—why God acts sometimes and not others. But ours is not a God who stands off and leaves us to suffer alone. Instead, he does as Elisha, meeting us on the altar of our dreams, stretching over us, and covering us with his love. It is a love that gives us hope for tomorrow, for miraculously, it is a love that can bring life out of death. That kind of love grounds our actions, compelling us to remain faithful—even courageous—in the midst of unfavorable odds.

The downfall of VeggieTales reminds us that God does not always respond to our prayers in the ways we want. But the larger point is that we are called not to be successful, only faithful. The English word *courage* emerged from the Old French *corage,* which referred to the heart or innermost feelings. Over time the term came to be associated with bravery and steadfastness. Sometimes courage requires closing down the business you started or ending an unhealthy relationship. Other times it entails not losing heart in the face of tragedy or great loss. Rarely can we foresee where a given situation will wind up, but daily acts of faithfulness lay the foundation for us to exemplify fortitude when the hinge moment entails closing a door, even one we wished could remain open.

## TEMPER MORE THAN YOUR TEMPER

Temperance, or proper and reasonable self-restraint, has meaning beyond the mere acknowledgement of "everything in moderation." It's also much more than avoiding intoxication, promiscuity, or gluttony. In fact, the Christian tradition has long attributed virtues like forgiveness and humility—with all the discipline they entail—as falling within the realm of temperance. In some sense, forgiveness is self-control turned outward. It is the restraint of your potential anger toward another person. Likewise, humility is self-control turned inward. It is the ability to control your own ego—to check your personal sense of importance. The Romans likened proper self-restraint to a recognition of humankind's interconnection. Emperor Marcus Aurelius put it this way:

> The wrongdoer has a nature related to my own! Not of blood
> or birth but of the same mind, and possessing a share of the

divine. . . . I cannot be angry at my relative, nor hate him, we were built to work together feet, hands and eyes, like the two rows of teeth, upper and lower. To obstruct each other is unnatural. To feel anger at someone, to turn your back on him: these are unnatural.[1]

Temperance in relation to others recognizes their humanity and the obligations you have toward them. Temperance in relation to yourself demands recognition that the rules apply to you too and that all good things have their proper time and measure. This sort of self-control concerns not only the affairs of our daily lives. There are times when the exercise of temperance requires a much larger and panoptic perspective.

October 27, 1962 was the day the world almost ended. One man, Vasili Arkhipov, displayed an act of temperance that should forever be remembered. Arkhipov was the second-in-command of the Soviet submarine B-59 during the Cuban missile crisis. Located deep underwater near Cuba and unable to receive outside communication due to mandated radio silence, the crew had not heard anything from Moscow in days when they were detected by the US Navy. The Americans released explosives intended to force B-59 to the surface. The crew was unsure how to proceed. Battery power in the submarine was dwindling, and the extreme heat in the vessel became unbearable. Some members of the crew suspected that war had broken out and wanted to launch nuclear warheads toward the US mainland to aid the Soviet offensive. Of course, if war had not broken out, this action would certainly begin one and likely result in global devastation. The captain and the third-in-command both wanted to launch the missile. But Soviet protocol required that all three officers make the unanimous decision to strike, and Arkhipov wanted to think about it. He eventually decided, much to the dismay of some of the crew, that no, he wouldn't agree to the launch but instead would wait for orders.

As Arkhipov's cooler head prevailed, the sub surfaced. The US Navy surrounded them and forced them to return to the Soviet Union in shame. For years Arkhipov endured taunts in his home country for choosing to surface. However, in 2002 Robert McNamara, the former US Secretary of Defense, and Arthur M. Schlesinger Jr., an advisor for the Kennedy administration, both publicly acknowledged that Arkhipov's decision prevented a nuclear war at "the most dangerous moment in human history."[2] Arkhipov is a notable example of someone who displayed temperance despite direct pressure to do the opposite.

Self-control saved civilization back in 1962, and it continues to serve us well in everyday life. Sociologist Bradley Wright and neuroscientist David Carreon have found that people with more self-control "live longer, are happier, get better grades, are less depressed, are more physically active, have lower resting heart rates, have less alcohol abuse, have more stable emotions, are more helpful to others, get better jobs, earn more money, have better marriages, are more faithful in marriage, and sleep better at night."[3]

Self-control is like a character muscle, one that gets stronger as it is used more regularly. Insights from brain research reveal three approaches that strengthen it. First, we have to substitute one instinctive response for another—choosing to pray with trust in God's goodness rather than to worry, for example, in moments of anxiety. This means that we deplete our ability to resist temptation with every exercise of self-control, so we have to develop endurance to resist over time. Reciting words of memorized Scripture when you see something that elicits lust can be a way to strengthen self-control, but it will be harder to do that if you have just spent time and energy resisting warm brownies as they come out of the oven. This leads to the second insight: practice regular rest. "A good night's sleep bolsters self-control the entire next day," Wright and Carreon found.[4] Regular exercise, a healthy diet, and sufficient rest not only contribute to overall wellness but they also strengthen your ability to demonstrate more temperance. Finally, identify small aspects of a larger behavioral change you are seeking and focus on *one* of these aspects at a time. The smaller, the better. As you master one piece of a larger shift you are trying to make possible, your brain sees the microadjustment as routine, requiring little effort or willpower. Gradually, you can string a series of these small adjustments together and, in the process, develop a new habit with much greater self-control "muscle memory." This in turn strengthens your self-control, permitting you to resist even greater temptation and reinforcing your overall ability to overcome.

New Testament scholar N. T. Wright connects this process of temperance development with the larger work of virtuous living:

> Virtue . . . is what happens when someone has made a thousand small choices requiring effort and concentration to do something which is good and right, but which doesn't "come naturally"—and then, on the thousand and first time, when it really matters, they find that they do what's required "automatically." . . . Virtue is what happens when wise and courageous choices become second nature.[5]

## JUSTICE: WHAT LOVE LOOKS LIKE IN PUBLIC

Aristotle and other pagan philosophers tended toward a relatively simple characterization of our fourth virtue: "Justice consists in a certain equality by which the just and definite claim of another, neither more nor less, is satisfied."[6] That is a sturdy explanation, but perhaps the best definition of justice is even simpler: giving people what they are due. This plays out most often in cases where dueling understandings of right and wrong call for a ruling by a disinterested third party. Then, equal cases (as with two adults) should be treated equally, and unequal cases (as with an adult and a child) should be treated with equity. So, if we can agree that justice means rendering to people what they are due, there are only two questions left: which of us are "people," and what are we due?

The first question may seem strange, but a casual glance down the historical timeline reveals that the scope of who *is* and *is not* a person has changed dramatically over the centuries. Humans have been playing identity politics for a long time. The category of "full person" shrinks as we head backward in history, excluding, for instance, at one point or another: women, people of color, foreigners, infidels, the lower classes, and sometimes disabled persons and the unborn. Since prehistory, tribal, ethnic, and national identities have determined (and limited) who counts as a person and what they are due. Even today we struggle with racism and classism and how they shape our understanding of justice.

In the West, it is not until the rise of Christianity that we start to see the concept that all people have worth because they are created in the image of God. Yet "love your neighbor as you love yourself" was not the revolutionary concept. That idea far predates Christianity and Judaism and is in fact ingrained in us naturally. Love of the family (or kinsman) is innate and biological. Jesus did not need to convince people to love their neighbor. When neighbor means fellow Israelite, love is easy, because we're talking about members of the tribe.

The brilliance of Jesus's commandment was revealed in his response to the question, "Who is my neighbor?" (Luke 10:29). With his answer in the form of the parable of the good Samaritan, he extended the boundaries of the tribe to include others not only outside of it but opposed to it. Suddenly, all people are now "your neighbor," and the commandment "Love your neighbor as you love yourself" takes on a whole new meaning.

Jesus knew that "loving" your neighbor was one thing but acting it out toward your neighbor was another. So as for what others are due, he was clear: we should treat all others, in every circumstance, as we would want to be treated. I think the King James Version has the best wording for this one: "Therefore all things whatsoever ye would that men should do to you, do ye even so to them" (Matthew 7:12 KJV). This, says Jesus, is the whole of the law and the prophets. The Christian understanding of justice, then, is by no means opaque. All people are your neighbors, and you should render to your neighbors exactly what it is you would want if you were in their shoes.

The parable of the good Samaritan has seven scenes, each pointing toward the center of the story, where the gospel mandate for justice is most clearly revealed. In scene one, the robbers take all the man's possessions, and in scene seven, the Samaritan pays out of his own resources for the man's care because the man needs a safe place to recuperate. In scene two, the priest fails to transport the wounded man to safety, and in scene six, the Samaritan fulfills that costly act, carrying him to a local inn. The Levite in scene three could have at least bound up the man's wounds, and in the matching scene five, the Samaritan compensates for this failure. The center of the parable in scene four describes the Samaritan's compassion: "A Samaritan, as he traveled, came where the man was; and when he saw him, he took pity on him" (Luke 10:33). Seven scenes in all. The climax—where true justice occurs—is at the center, and the last three scenes are linked to the first three in an inverted order.[7]

In the oral culture of the ancient Near East, where messages were typically spoken rather than written down, stories that establish a series also set a direction. If a contemporary story were to begin with a character of governor, and then a senator, then we might expect the next level character to be the president. The story could also go in reverse order. It could begin with the pope, and then introduce a bishop, and likely the third character would be a priest. If a first-century Jewish story introduces a Hebrew priest, then a Levite, the third person down the road should be a Jewish layman. After all, those are the three classes of religious workers at that time: priests, Levites, and laymen. But that is not what happens in this story; instead, Jesus tells a far more scandalous story where justice enters in a surprising way.

You see, it would have been acceptable to the audience if Jesus had told a story about a good Jew who helped a Samaritan. But it's an entirely different story when Jesus introduces the third character not as a good Jewish laymen but instead a good Samaritan. This is so tough for the lawyer (who had asked Jesus the question, "Who is my neighbor?") to accept that he cannot respond directly to Jesus' question about which of the three was a neighbor to the man who fell into the hands of the robbers. He answers Jesus with an oblique reference to the Samaritan without naming him: "The one who had mercy on him" (Luke 10:37).

In this conversation with Jesus, the lawyer is given a standard that he knows he cannot meet. In the process, he discovers that he cannot earn eternal life, for it comes to him as a free gift. The challenge for him and for all of us is to pursue justice by responding with sacrificial love to meet the needs of those God puts in our paths. As American philosopher Cornel West has stated numerous times, "Justice is what love looks like in public."

This, therefore, is the distinctive life hinge of the Christian faith. You will find in other religions and philosophies various calls to wisdom, self-control, and courage, but the expansion of rights and justice to all people of all tribes is rare. If trusted and held tightly, this understanding will be an anchoring hinge for you in transitions and will provide a framework for the proper treatment of all those you will meet in your new space. Many might not seem at all like your "neighbor." You might not even recognize some of their tastes, habits, or priorities. You would do well to have a sturdy hinge for yourself that requires that you treat those people the way Jesus commanded—like neighbors worthy of their Creator's love and yours. And you should hope for your sake that they have a similar view of you.

# 7

# PASSAGES

## GROWING THROUGH MAJOR LIFE CHANGES

*Remember not the former things,*
*nor consider the things of old.*
*Behold, I am doing a new thing;*
*now it springs forth, do you not perceive it?*
*I will make a way in the wilderness*
*and rivers in the desert.*

ISAIAH 43:18-19 ESV

CLASSICAL ECONOMIC THEORY had long assumed that human beings were rational actors who used all the information we had to weigh options and make decisions that corresponded to our expectation for maximum utility (a term only economists would use to mean general happiness and well-being). It was also thought that we viewed gain and loss in equal and absolute terms. In other words, losing ten dollars would change our happiness in one direction by the same amount proportionally that gaining ten dollars would change it in the other direction. It turns out this is not even close to reality: we are loss-averse creatures.

Research pioneered by Daniel Kahneman, the psychologist introduced in chapter two, suggests that our fear of losing things is roughly twice as strong as our desire to gain them. Losing a sum of money hurts twice as badly as the happiness we get from gaining that same sum.[1] This fear-of-loss principle can be seen in the example of the coin-toss experiment also described in chapter two. When we are close to making a good decision, we are still timid about shouldering the burden alone and want the safety net of another's opinion, even if it's only a random coin toss.

Fear of loss can include fear of failure, which can keep us from grabbing hold of a great opportunity because we are scared we aren't qualified or won't be impressive. In these moments, when we are weighing the potential losses and gains, we need to remember that embarrassment and failure are not terminal illnesses. We get over them (like bad colds) and grow stronger from them (as our immune system does) if we're willing to cross the threshold.

Eventually, we reach the final stage of a transition: *realization.* Here the benefits of our growth and development come to fulfillment, producing greater maturity and strength in our character and lives.

> We need to remember that embarrassment and failure are not terminal illnesses.

In some cases, the transition will leave scars of some kind, but with those scars come powerful stories—stories of recovery, redemption, and maybe even resurrection. Moreover, having moved through the stages of transition, our overall confidence has grown, making it more manageable to face similar or lesser changes in our future, or—if faced with an even tougher change down the road—we have gained wisdom, experience, and strength for the journey ahead.

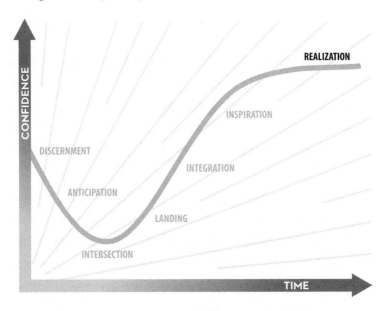

## RESPONDING TO HARD JOYS

In my own life, I have found the hardest hinge moments have become the most important crucibles for growth and character building. When my oldest daughter, Elizabeth, was four months old, we began to sense that something wasn't quite right with her developmentally. Over the next several months, we tried various tactics to help her catch up and eventually took her to see an experienced pediatrician. On that warm September afternoon, the doctor spent nearly half an hour examining Elizabeth, occasionally asking us questions while poking and prodding and then watching for certain responses. She was holding my heart in her hands as she held my baby girl.

Eventually, the doctor handed Elizabeth back to my wife and then cleared her throat: "Well, I don't know what to say, but something is definitely wrong with your little girl." She continued to speak for a few minutes, but I had stopped listening. In that sterile examining room, I found it difficult to breathe. When we got to our car, we could barely speak to our parents over the cell phone; grief overtook us and made it hard to get out even basic words. In the hours that followed, Rebecca and I agonized and grieved the loss of a future we had never articulated but felt entitled to. Every new bit of data or piece of information we received over the following days and weeks seemed worse than the last. We prayed hard that our worst fears wouldn't live themselves out, but we dreaded that they would. For the next two years, we took Elizabeth to see a variety of specialists, none of whom were able to identify an underlying condition or a possible treatment for her.

It would not be until Elizabeth was three years old that an assistant professor of genetics at Baylor College of Medicine would identify an extremely rare genetic disorder that, it turns out, my wife and I (and our families) are carriers for. Elizabeth is one of five hundred or so known cases in the world. There is no cure, and it is a complicated disorder that entails profound cognitive disability (with no real language to speak of), dangerously low white blood cell count, legal blindness, and many challenges with internal organs. If you look at Elizabeth from afar, you assume she is typical, but if you interact with her for even a few seconds, you realize that she is very special. Communicating with Elizabeth is a great challenge and caring for her has become a journey of obedience in our lives. The hinge moment occurred that September afternoon when Rebecca and

I had to decide how we would process this unexpected turn in the life of our family. In the intervening years (Elizabeth is now sixteen), we have experienced many moments of satisfying joy in parenting her. But at other times, it has been more like a heavy joy, a hard joy.

The point of the Christian life is transformation. Parenting Elizabeth has taught us important lessons. She is not drawn to the seductive sirens of status or fame or self-advancement. And as such, she reflects a more authentic way of Christian living, one that is less interested in appearances or achievement.

She takes great pleasure in simple things—the taste of vanilla ice cream, the thrill of reaching heights in a backyard swing, the delight of listening to songs with a good beat and familiar melody. And Elizabeth is genuinely happy when she pleases her father, clapping for herself when she hears my affirmations and knows she has done something right. Having Elizabeth in our family has made visible for each of us the importance of vulnerability and simple obedience as part of the Christian journey. Moreover, she has demonstrated that walking "in a manner worthy of the Lord," as Paul puts it in Colossians 1:10, relies not on erudition or even specific behaviors. Instead, it is a disposition—a way of being—that opens us up to fully pleasing the Lord in our respective callings.

My wife and I began the process of learning all this through that fateful hinge moment, and it has reoriented our entire lives. But even though this *change* wasn't one that we chose, our *transition* has been all about choices. We choose to allow God to shape and bless us through difficulty, and we traded in our dream for our firstborn for his dream instead.

## TAKE A CHANCE AND FORCE
## YOUR WAY FORWARD

When Colleen Barrett was thirty-four, she was a single parent without a driver's license, working as a legal secretary in San Antonio, Texas. She was in many ways more economically vulnerable than most. She would travel from city to city, providing administrative support for Herb Kelleher, the attorney for whom she worked. She recalled for me how one day the two of them had gone to Dallas for an emergency meeting with a company for which Herb was a board member. The previous president of the company had decided to step down suddenly—in a grand gesture he had thrown the office keys on his desk and walked out the door. The company was suddenly in desperate need of a new leader. The board named Kelleher president and, because she was standing there, they made Barrett the corporate secretary. She accepted this new, unnerving career change, pressing forward despite fears of failure.

The company in question was a small regional carrier known as Southwest Airlines, and that was the start of Barrett's career in commercial aviation. Not only did she stay on when she easily might have backed away but she leaned into the opportunity, participating more and more in this new role that had opened up for her so quickly. Fast forward a few decades and Colleen Barrett became the first woman ever to serve as the president of a major airline. Not only that but under her watch Southwest grew to be the largest domestic carrier in the United States and the most profitable venture in aviation history.

Barrett's decision to take on a leadership role for which she was educationally unqualified was surely a gamble. But what was the worst that could have happened? She wasn't risking her own capital or putting herself in some mortal danger. She was only at risk of failure. So she chose to make the most of the opportunity.

Her virtues and values rose to the top alongside her. She revolutionized the company's culture by treating people with great care and displaying overflowing generosity toward her employees. She had been given a chance to succeed, and she passed that chance on to the hard workers below her. Consequently, Southwest developed an enviable corporate culture where employees went to extraordinary lengths to serve one another and their customers. Barrett told me how employees would come to her asking for personal loans or other favors, knowing that she would help them if she could. She even once delayed selling her home so that she could honor a promise made to a flight attendant who wanted to hold her wedding in Colleen's backyard.

Barrett's story is marked by two guiding principles for maximizing the value of transitions: take a chance and force your way forward. She took a chance by staying on with a small regional carrier based six hours from her home, and she asserted herself, forcing her way forward, even as she had a fair measure of self-doubt. She did not force her way *up* with the ruthlessness of someone like Hank Greenberg from AIG. She advanced not by stepping on others to get to the top but by pursuing promotion while treating the people around her (and below her) with kindness and generosity, thereby earning their trust and commitment. In this way, Barrett leveraged a serendipitous moment into a lifelong career at a company that she helped build from the ground up.

Looking at her career today, you might assume that Colleen Barrett had it all figured out at the outset. In reality, she responded to the opportunities that were before her as they came. So it is with most outstanding leaders. In fact, most exemplars in the Bible are individuals who responded not to one major hinge moment in their lives but to a series of such moments as each arose. Joseph had no idea the journey he would eventually take as he taunted his brothers about his father's affection and that special coat. And as he was sold into slavery, he had no premonition that this would become the means by which he would eventually rise to be a trusted advisor to the pharaoh—but only after he rebuffed the advances of Potiphar's wife and ended up being falsely imprisoned. At the end of his story, Joseph harbors no ill will toward his brothers or resentment for the journey he undertook. "You intended to harm me," he tells his brothers, "but God intended it all for good" (Genesis 50:20 NLT). That sense of learning and growing through each of the hinge moments that we face turns out to be the key to a good end.

Or look at the apostle Peter, who faced a hinge moment when his faith in Christ was sorely tested against what he thought he knew about the Messiah. Following Christ's death, resurrection, and ascension, Peter still had much to learn about what the new church was going to look like. He has a vision where God tells him multiple times to eat food that had been considered up to this point strictly forbidden for the Jews. Peter argues back that God must be mistaken here: "Surely not, Lord!" Peter points out that he would have to make a complete one-eighty pivot in order to adopt this new way of thinking about food and spirituality: "I have never eaten anything impure or unclean" (Acts 10:14).

The Scriptures seem to portray Peter as ambivalent at this point. I imagine that even though he knew the vision had been from God, he felt helpless and confused. He wanted to be obedient, but what would he tell the other apostles? How could everything change from what he had known was true since he was a boy? The Scriptures say that he "was wondering" and "still thinking about the vision," just like we do when our own hinge moments come. Like Rebecca and me when we heard the confusing, terrifying words from the doctor about Elizabeth's condition, Peter no doubt felt stunned and unsure.

But then God stepped in with a new message to Peter: "Do not hesitate to go with them, for I have sent them" (Acts 10:20). In this case, God wanted Peter to go with some men who had just arrived at the door, whom he would follow the next day to the house of a Gentile. But this was not just any Gentile; he was a Roman centurion. That day Peter would, for the first time ever, preach the gospel to a complete outsider, and he would see the man's whole family and group of friends believe in Christ. Peter realized that he was making a pivot like nothing he had known before: "You are well aware that it is against our law for a Jew to associate with or visit a Gentile," he said to the centurion. "But God has shown me that I should not call anyone impure or unclean" (Acts 10:28).

Everything changed that day for Peter, for all the believers in the early church, and for the future of Christianity itself. All because Peter was not too afraid to pivot and because he was willing to trust God even when it seemed like his whole world was turning upside down. In the same way, your hinge moments can seem like God doesn't know what he's doing: "Surely not, Lord!" But when you realize that God is calling you to something new, even way out of your comfort zone, his message to you is like his message to Peter: "Do not hesitate, for I have sent this."

## FAILURE IS LEARNING

Sometimes even when we are trying our best to listen to the voice of God and follow his directions, our efforts seem to bear no good fruit. These are times when God is teaching us invaluable lessons. Irish philosopher and politician Edmund Burke once said, "Example is the school of mankind, and they will learn at no other."[2] He was right. Certain things can only be taught by experience on the job and in the midst of life's inevitable transitions. These transitions provide unrivaled lessons that serve us well for the rest of life. Colleen Barrett's path toward the presidency of a Fortune 500 company was not typical; she did not go to the best schools or run in the usual executive circles. She learned in a more informal but no less legitimate way through experience in transitions.

I do not know exactly just how many transitions you will have in your life, and you may never have a break quite like Barrett's. But all of us, no matter our station, are given opportunities, and I am certain you will fail in some of them. But risking failure is the only way to have a shot at any of the big breaks that can end up being so meaningful. In fact, failure can be our greatest teacher and source of example for what not to do next time. In this sense, a failure at one transition can equip us for life's next hinge moment, and pressure or challenge that arises from failure can become one of the most important teachers for what lies ahead.

Diamonds are the hardest known substance and are among the greatest conductors of heat on earth. They have the highest melting point of anything we've discovered—from four thousand to seven thousand degrees (F). They have the densest atomic configuration of any mineral, and they are transparent over the greatest number of wavelengths. These unique qualities are why diamonds are so precious and valued in the world, but they develop through an intense process.

Diamond crystals form deep within the mantle of the earth when carbon molecules are exposed to extreme pressure and very high temperature. If there is no pressure, the carbon forms graphite—a common substance not nearly as brilliant or impressive as diamond. It is the unique combination of intense pressure and high temperature that produces the diamond crystal. And the particulars of each diamond's experience are what distinguish one from another, giving them varying degrees of color and clarity. So it is with each of us. Failure and challenge refine us in ways that success and ease simply cannot. Virtually every person who successfully navigates the most important hinge moments of life experiences misses and disappointments along the way, but these people recognize that failure doesn't have to be final.

> Failure and challenge refine us in ways that success and ease simply cannot.

Bruce Dunlevie, a wildly successful venture capitalist, provided early funding for a number of companies that have produced tech products you and I use every day. But before he was a titan of industry, he was the new guy at a venture capital firm. He and I spoke about how seasons of failure had been extremely formative for his career and how much he had learned from them. As a young and eager investor, he had set his heart on making the first company he invested in into a success. Everything was going perfectly: the product was great, he loved the management team, and the company looked like it was poised to expand. He was on top of the world with how well things seemed to be going. Then one day he walked in for a meeting and learned that everything was falling apart. It turned out that all the financial partner prospects had dried up, and the company was left with no cash reserves. Within a short time the business was dissolved. Dunlevie was shattered by what he experienced as a personal failure. But a more senior mentor at his firm saw this as a propitious teaching moment. He knew that many people think they are going to bat a thousand in venture capital, but in reality no one even bats five hundred. This mentor laughingly told Dunlevie that having such an early failure was "the cheapest tuition ever" for learning the skills for investing.

Indeed, I have found that failures in transitionary periods need not be setbacks or wasted time but opportunities to "fail forward," propelling us toward the next transition and future success. In the lives of virtually every great person I met in the PLATINUM study, such failing forward provided an opportunity for reinvestment and reorientation. They did not always understand this at the time when the bottom fell out, but later they would look back and label these moments the key inflection points of their lives.

In the same way that we must work against our innate risk aversion, so also must we be open to the idea that our current pursuit may not be working out for us. One of the ways we grow the most from hinge moments is to learn how to leverage them when a transition needs to come, whether we want it or not. As

> Failures in transitionary periods need not be setbacks or wasted time but opportunities to "fail forward," propelling us toward the next transition and future success.

soon as we set out to launch something, we often want so badly
for it to be the right thing that we are unwilling to admit when the
results are not as they ought to be. Because of this, we can fall prey
to that sunk-cost fallacy: we argue that because we have already
invested so much time, effort, and resources into something (our
"sunk costs"), it is worth our while to keep investing in it and hope
that it works. This subconscious calculation can clog up our good
thinking, so that we are essentially continuing to bail water out of
a flooding house. Sometimes we've just got to grab what we can,
cut our losses, and evacuate.

No one wants to admit that a chance taken or a transition made
is not getting them anywhere good. But sometimes that is the best
thing you can do to set yourself up for the next opportunity, af-
fording yourself the chance for longer range success. Dunlevie's
philosophy is that in real life, many ventures will not turn out the
way you wanted. The most important—and in his words, "courageous"—thing is to realize that you are not going to "in our eyes
or anybody else's eyes, be viewed as failures if [you] decide to pack
this one up and go play another game somewhere else." This is
why we never burn the ships when we make a transition. You may
need to ride them back home when plans sour. Historically, there
have been a lot of people who chose, for good reason, to get back
in their boats and return to where their journey began.

Between 1850 and 1914, millions of people immigrated to the
United States from Europe, hoping to make a new home for themselves and their families. They came for a number of reasons:
religious liberty, fleeing turmoil in their homelands, or simply the
chance for a better life. It is difficult for us to even imagine the
colossal scale of the risk they took in making this move. Many

arrived with little or no money at all. Many did not speak the language. They often came with little formal education, and most of them had no idea what their lives would look like once they stepped off the boat on the other side of the Atlantic. This story is familiar history to us, but what is less known is that one in three of these immigrants eventually returned home.[3] It is difficult to imagine the pressure they must have felt to remain in the United States no matter the challenges, yet they had to go back to their homelands. But was this a failure for them?

Amid their difficulties in the United States, they had learned skills, mastered important virtues (like perseverance), and hopefully saved up some money. Maybe they went back inspired, wiser, more confident in their risk-taking abilities. For whatever reason, scholarship has revealed, most of the returning immigrants ended up thriving back home. They often earned higher wages and had higher-skilled occupations than their neighbors who had never moved.[4] They may have failed in their goal of immigrating to America, but they were able to leverage that failure into a prosperous future when they chose to course correct.

The fact is that failures teach unique skills and bestow unique resources that simply cannot be acquired otherwise. If we believe that "in all things God works for the good of those who love him" (Romans 8:28)—and that God has a controlling hand in all human affairs—then we have to accept that ultimately nothing is left to chance. Even changes we make and risks we take that end up not working out can contribute toward something meaningful in our lives later on. As Frederick Buechner puts it, "Even the saddest things can become, once we have made peace with them, a source of wisdom and strength for the journey that still lies ahead."[5]

Part of the redemption that occurs in failure, disappointment, pressure, and challenge arises from the way that God uses these seasons to grow us into better people. Far too often, we are like Jonah who, having been given a command to preach to his enemies, "ran away from the LORD" (Jonah 1:3). This proud man had no intention of complicating his life and watching the very people that he hated receive grace from God. But then, as the story goes, he found himself in the belly of a whale. From there he prayed:

> When my life was ebbing away,
>> I remembered you, LORD,
> and my prayer rose to you. (Jonah 2:7)

Seasons of great confinement or challenge often yield moments of great clarity.

This was true for virtually every person I researched, all 550 of them. Their challenge may have come in the form of a lost job, a lost child, or a lost dream. Sometimes it took place in public view; often, it occurred in private. But for virtually everyone, there were moments of deep introspection and reckoning. For Jonah, it took place in the belly of a whale. In some cultures, this image has become axiomatic to understanding how we are able to proclaim the gospel. In Eastern Europe, for instance, there is a tradition in which the pulpit is fashioned like an upright whale. The preacher climbs up to the pulpit on a set of stairs that go through its belly and then delivers the sermon from its open mouth.[6] This serves as a visible reminder that God's message penetrates the most when we are most attentive, and sometimes that can only occur when we are trapped somewhere *very* uncomfortable.

## WHEN MOVING UP IS NOT THE RIGHT MOVE

Of course, not every possible transition is the right one. Remember that we are a cautious and risk-averse species for a reason. This trait is in part a result of the way our ancestors survived over time. Wisdom requires that we view opportunities as they come and decide what is best for us and for those around us. How can you know if the doorway opened to you is the wrong one? Check your motives, check with your family and others who care about you, and ask God for guidance.

Healthcare executive Joel Allison was leading a small hospital system in Amarillo, Texas, and doing a great job. Others were noticing his expertise, and his career was on a fast track for greater opportunity. Everyone expected he would someday soon move to Dallas or Houston to lead one of the larger health systems there. One day, however, he was offered a position as the head of a small children's hospital in Corpus Christi—a major step backward on the career ladder. Outside observers assumed he would dismiss the idea immediately. But Allison is a man of faith, and he was more interested in what God thought.

After extended consideration and prayer, he and his wife decided that it would be best for their family to move to this coastal city, about one-seventh the size of Houston. Many in the industry thought he was destroying his career prospects. But by his own account, the move "didn't hurt me one bit. I did it for the right reason. I did it for the family. . . . And it was the best decision I ever made. And again . . . it was God's plan. It was God's will." There was seemingly no professional benefit to Allison's decision to make this move, but it was the transition his family needed at the time, and his value of family health ran deeper than his value of fame and fortune.

As the Lord would have it, Allison's success in Corpus Christi exposed him to other statewide opportunities. Governor Rick Perry appointed him to the state Healthcare Leadership Council. Eventually, he was offered headship of what became Baylor Scott & White, a system that includes forty-eight hospitals, more than nine hundred patient-care sites, more than six thousand active physicians, and more than forty thousand employees. By the time this job offer came, a step into a big-time career and all it entailed was now the right choice for him and his family.

A straight line of career advancement is not required for everyone who rises to the top. Sometimes the best move is a quiet one with no immediately obvious payout. But as Allison found, those with talent and capability are often given additional opportunities for career advancement. Hinge moments come to us many times over the course of our lives. Yes, you must take full advantage of each one, but sometimes the best advantage comes from saying a confident and well-considered, "No, thank you."

Transitions like the ones Colleen Barrett, Bruce Dunlevie, and Joel Allison underwent are different in starting point and destination, but they are the same in that they revealed something about the people crossing the thresholds of change. Barrett's tenacity and kindheartedness were the shining lights of her success. Dunlevie had to display humility and patience to move on from his early failures. Allison's sincere love for his family and for God were revealed through his career decisions.

Because transitions are difficult, we can be tempted either to rush through them or pretend they will not come at all. But experience shows that we all will face these significant and pivotal moments around which the rest of our life hinges. The goal of preparing for such transitions is to maximize their teachable possibilities and to leverage them for the greatest good in our lives and the lives of others.

In hindsight, it is easy to pick out the turning points that shaped the trajectories of our lives. But it is not so easy in real time. Sometimes these moments announce themselves as they approach, and other times we suddenly find ourselves knee-deep in living-room flood waters that lead us to entirely new futures. When that happens, it will be too late to get ready. The only way to respond is to trust that the disciplines we have been practicing and the values and virtues we have cultivated will, with God's help, serve us well in the moment as we weigh our options and move forward. As we do that, with a little grit and a lot of faith, the hurdles that so often accompany transitions will be less challenging for us, and we will rightly see the changes in our lives for what they are: our own hinge moments.

# CONCLUSION

CONDOLEEZZA RICE HAD SPENT virtually her whole life through her sophomore year in college on a piano bench, working toward a professional music career. That summer she went to study and perform at the Aspen Music Festival, a prestigious and competitively sought honor. While there, she came into contact with, as she put it, "eleven-year-olds who could play from sight what had taken me all year to learn." She knew that she could not compete with people of such innate talent. She knew she would never be the best, and that meant this wasn't the path she wanted to pursue. At the start of her junior year, she changed her major from music to international relations. And the rest is history.

Rice earned graduate degrees in political science from Notre Dame and would go on to become an expert on the Soviet Union and eventually foreign policy. She served as the national security advisor and then US secretary of state (as the first woman of color to do so). Her life (and the future lives of countless others) was changed that fateful day when nineteen-year-old "Condi" decided she would not be a pianist. She didn't waste time staring at a door that was closing but instead, while the opportunity was still ripe, pushed a new one open.

The ancient Greeks had two words for time: *chronos* and *kairos*. Chronos is time as we typically think of it: linear (hence "chronological"), gradual, and predictable. Your watch and cellphone measure chronos as it passes. Kairos, however, is less measured than it is *recognized*. The word translates to "opportune time." It is the moment when luck or fate (or the gods, in the Greeks' case) brings an opportunity your way but only for a fleeting moment. When depicted in art, Kairos wore long hair on his forehead but was bald in the back. He was often shown sprinting. According to the myth, when he was asked why he had such an unusual haircut, his answer emphasized his ephemeral nature: "Because none whom I have once raced by on my winged feet will now, though he wishes it sore, take hold of me from behind."[1] The ancient Greeks had such a clever way of depicting the intangibles. It is true: opportunities will often come rushing by, and if you wait until after they pass to grab hold of them, you'll usually find yourself empty-handed. The moment of kairos is, in a word, precious.

The New Testament, originally written in Greek, uses the word *chronos* fifty-four times, usually to denote a certain time or span of time. *Kairos* is used eighty-six times and denotes a special opportunity. Often the Gospel writers would even juxtapose the two words for effect. For instance, in John 5, when Jesus heals the man at the pool of Bethesda, our Lord learns that the man had been lame for quite a long while (*chronos*), waiting for the time (*kairos*) when he could be healed. The man at the pool did not wake up knowing that this would be the day of his healing, the day *kairos* would come sprinting by. Neither did Condoleezza Rice know that her discouragement in Aspen would set her on a path toward becoming secretary of state. Hindsight will make clear for you when *kairos* came for you; you can't always see it when it happens. But you can make sure that your hinges are strong, ready to pivot at a moment's notice.

Your personal qualities and character are like hinges on a door: they will either be strong and ready, preparing you to pivot perfectly, or they will be feeble and so essentially useless.

Condoleezza Rice's confidence and ability to pivot in her hinge moment was grounded in her faith in Jesus Christ. Many doors had been closed in her face while growing up in segregated Birmingham, Alabama, but she never let that stop her. Her hinges had been well kept, and she was ready when her hinge moment came. So it must be for us.

## BEING READY

There are transitions that allow for time to think, and there are those that hit you like a ton of bricks, challenging you to react and testing your courage and character in an instant. But all transitions—even voluntary ones like a job offer or celebratory ones like a long-awaited pregnancy—begin with change. As I said earlier, only one thing remains the same: the fact that nothing does. You can't control everything (or much of anything) that happens to you, but you can choose how you respond to those changes and how you manage the transitions you walk through in the process. Small, incremental changes can also become proving grounds for much larger, more challenging turns in your life.

As we process these changes, we move through seven stages of transition—discernment (when we decide if it's the right move), anticipation (when we actively prepare for the move), intersection (when we stand in the threshold between our past and our future), landing (when we are actively learning our new way of life), integration (when we develop ties of trust and mutual support), inspiration (when we begin to make sense of the change and use that to help and inspire others), and realization (when the benefits of the change come to fulfillment).

It's virtually impossible to stand in the present moments of your life and predict what will happen in the days and years ahead. Each new threshold you cross and home you enter will produce consequences for what happens to you over the rest of your life. Never doubt the manifold possibilities God could have in store for you. As Ephesians 2:10 reminds us, we were "created in Christ Jesus to do good works, which God prepared in advance for us to do." Part of the thrill and excitement of changes in our lives is that they afford us new opportunities to do good.

Thomas Lake is a relatively unassuming, homeschooled son of a pastor. He, along with five siblings, spent part of his childhood in a small town in Georgia. Anyone standing by at the day of his birth trying to guess where his life would take him would have guessed wrong. Over the years, he developed a passion for the written word and for telling stories well. Through school newspapers and other outlets, he honed his ability to write well and communicate in a way that gripped the hearts and minds of his readers. By the ripe old age of thirty (when many people are just starting their careers) he was named a senior writer for *Sports Illustrated* and was hailed by many as *the* best sportswriter in the United States. He won the Henry Luce Award for most outstanding story of 2009 across all Time publications for his first magazine story, "2 on 5." Three years later his essay, "The Boy They Couldn't Kill," was named one of the sixty best features in the history of *Sports Illustrated.* By 2016, he was working for CNN Digital, championing their coverage of the presidential race and authoring *Unprecedented: The Election that Changed Everything.* Today, Tom is recognized as one of the premier young journalists in the United States and one of the few remaining masters of long form journalism.

But few would have predicted this would be Tom's journey. From reading the encyclopedia with his brother as a child, to his family's church involvement, to college at Gordon and beyond, it was never exactly clear where God was taking him. The imperceptibility of our future paths shrouds our lives in a fog. It's natural for that to feel scary, even ominous, at times. But the clear message spoken to so many in the Bible, "Do not be afraid," rings true for us as well. The Lord walks beside us in the high and low points of our journey and is at this very moment preparing something for us and preparing us for something as well.

## REDEMPTION THROUGH HINGE MOMENTS

The decade between age twenty and thirty are filled with hinge moments, and what happens during the college years typically exerts an outsized influence on the rest of their lives—for good or for bad. When Dan Bartlett (first introduced in chapter four) was in his early twenties, he was kicked off his college campus. He was a member of a fraternity at the University of Texas at Austin that had engaged in some hazing of pledges (which was, of course, contrary to the university's rules). As a result, all the fraternity members were suspended from school. This event could have easily been the introduction to the story of a life with a downward spiral. It is not difficult to imagine the tale of a young man who had a promising future that was dashed by some poor decisions. That sort of thing happens all the time. But that was not how it would be for Bartlett.

When he and I sat down for an interview, he referenced that specific moment of school suspension as the turning point of his life. He had grown up in a small town in Texas, gone to a rural high school, and by his own admission was not particularly driven, self-motivated, or concerned with the expectations of others. Getting kicked off campus might have been the end of his prospects. But instead it was a wake-up call. He realized that he needed to make a change in his life quickly. He resolved to find a job as soon as he could to occupy his time and to keep him out of trouble while he was suspended. In his search, he met Karl Rove, who was working on the George W. Bush gubernatorial campaign and liked Bartlett right away. A short ten years later, at age thirty-one, Barlett was named counselor to president for George W. Bush. He would serve in that role for five years, after which he would go on to serve at a number of institutions, including as an adjunct faculty member on the very campus from which he had once been suspended. Sometimes, hinge moments work together to complete a three-sixty, bringing us back to the place where we started. What others might use for bad, God can use for good.

Bartlett's rise to high office occurred through more than just his proper managing of an opportunity for transition. Not everyone will meet a senior political consultant while looking for a job. But the key takeaway from his story is that rather than sulk, or let the expectations of others define him, Bartlett took a major behavioral failure as a call to action. God often uses setback and disappointment as the crucible for our transformation. From Joseph to Esther to Peter, we see throughout the Bible stories of remarkable redemption, most often occurring after moments of grave injustice or intemperance. The difficulty Bartlett overcame was a psychological one. When we fail, either through our own devices or by the hand of external forces, the temptation to succumb to the expectations of that failure can be intense. But we must view failures in much the same way as successes. Neither is a guarantee of what is to come. Neither will fully define who or what you become. And the nature of the next chapter of your life depends on whether you are able to leverage all things, good and bad, for the benefit of your future trajectory. This is how God uses failure to help us grow and grow up.

When I think of radical transformations, my mind goes immediately to Saul of Tarsus. You can read his story in Acts 9. A blinding light stops him in his tracks on a journey to Damascus, and God the Son himself addresses him, calling for an end to his bloodthirsty persecution of Christians. He can never go back to who he was before. For Saul, there was no scouting ahead, weighing options, or making good first impressions. His change happened to him with no warning and no relenting.

After the *change*—you should know after reading this book—comes the *transition*. Saul has three days to think about his life's trajectory. Still blinded, he is stranded in Damascus, having to be led by the hand for everything. He can now do little more than think about his life. By the time Ananias is sent by God to heal him, Saul has chosen his response to the change that had been forced on him: he would cross the threshold of the door Christ had opened and become God's apostle to the Gentiles. We each, in God's providence, have a unique role to fulfill through our lives and our callings. We never know how the Lord will use our circumstances and our experiences to be a blessing to others, but the wonderful thing about our God is that he chooses to accomplish most of what he wants in the world through ordinary people like you and me.

✳   ✳   ✳

Corrie ten Boom showed remarkable courage in situations that are unfathomable to most of us. She was the first licensed watchmaker in Amsterdam, yet that is hardly why she is remembered today. She lived in the Netherlands at the height of World War II. Her father was passionate about helping Jews escape the Nazis, and it did not take long for his daughter to follow his example. Ten Boom built a secret room in her home to shelter fleeing Jews, and she installed a warning buzzer to alert them when Nazi patrols were near. She befriended government officials at the local office to get extra ration cards to feed the people concealed in her house, which became known to Jews as "the hiding place."

In 1944, she was arrested and tried for her actions. At her first hearing, Nazi lieutenants taunted her for helping not only Jews but also the mentally disabled (who were being killed in the name of "racial hygiene" and eugenics). Ten Boom famously stated that a mentally disabled person is far more valuable than any watchmaker—or lieutenant. (To a father of a special needs daughter, that declaration means a lot.)

She ended up being sent to a women's labor camp in Germany where she held worship services for the women, despite threats from the guards. Following her release and the end of the war, she continued her mission, opening a center to shelter concentration camp survivors.

Ten Boom's life story is an example of why it is so important not only to have hinges but to have *steady* hinges. Exercising virtue is easy when the days are sunny. For this reason, it is no problem for you or me to sit as you are now, reading this book in comfort and assuring ourselves that we would have had the fortitude of Corrie ten Boom. And perhaps we would have. But there were many other Christians in the Netherlands whose courage was *not* strong enough, and they indeed did nothing or even cooperated with the evil around them because of fear. The purpose of a steady and well-mounted hinge is to have it ready and set firmly *before* any pressure is applied. Use the time of peace and convenience to make sure your hinges are ready so that when the time for courage comes, you will not falter. We strengthen our hinges by practicing our faith regularly. This could mean giving generously to others (even before or in-between times when we have steady income) and resisting temptation in our life by, for instance, fasting from digital devices or finding accountability partners to help us avoid pornography or gossip. Indeed, the surest way to prepare for our uncertain future is to practice virtues that we want to embody when difficulties inevitably arise.

In sum, the way we respond to change is largely about the choices we make through the various stages of transition. We may not have control over much, but the way we respond to whatever occurs is one major way that we can embody virtue. Remarkably, it is through stages of transition that we develop the maturity and wisdom to handle changes as they come, and with each successive journey through the seven stages of transition, we emerge stronger and better. Ours is a God who works in and through the changes of life to shape our character and use us in ways that reflect God's glory. And the great gift of the life of faith is that God accompanies us on the journey; as Isaiah says, "This is the way; walk in it" (Isaiah 30:21).

# AFTERWORD

IN THE MIDST OF WRITING this book about the hinge moments in life, I began to wonder if God was preparing me for a moment of my own. At the time, I was enjoying my dream job—president of a nationally-ranked Christian college where, despite some challenges and setbacks, I felt God's pleasure and loved what I was doing. Nevertheless, the process of preparing me for the idea that my tenth year as Gordon's president might be my final one began one fall evening over dinner.

Arthur Brooks, a talented social scientist who successfully led the American Enterprise Institute in Washington, was talking to a group of Gordon supporters. We were seated together, and over the course of the meal, he explained his decision to step down as AEI's head after a decade in the role. I remembered being shocked when I first heard the news because his run there had been so successful, and everyone assumed he would be there until retirement. But as he shared the reasoning behind his decision with me I felt butterflies in my stomach, which was odd. Why would I be nervous for him or feel anxious about a decision he made for his own life? I came to recognize those internal feelings—ones that each of us have felt at various points in life—as an initial prompting of the Holy Spirit. But I must confess this was not an idea that I liked at all. I was happy and very engaged in my work at the time, our family was doing well, and all seemed right in the world.

A few months later, though, while researching this book, I encountered another divine prompting. I was reviewing the transcript of the research interview I had conducted years earlier with Bruce Kennedy, the one-time leader of Alaska Airlines. As I skimmed the pages, my eyes landed upon that part of the interview where Bruce discussed his decision to step down from the airline after ten years. Immediately, the butterflies returned.

In the days and weeks that followed, my wife and I talked at length, wondering aloud what God might be doing in all of this. Eventually, I had some conversations with the leadership of Gordon's Board of Trustees about stepping down at the end of my tenth year. Shortly thereafter, the coronavirus pandemic hit and we put those discussions aside. Gradually, however, Gordon's resilience emerged as we exited the emergency phase of the pandemic, and I began to see several things falling into place.

For one, I had worked almost my entire presidency toward a major step of making Gordon more affordable. And I realized that both the fundraising campaign and the strategic plan that I helped steward were likely to conclude by the end of what would be my tenth year on the job. So as the moment approached for Gordon to announce a tuition reset and the realization of those decade-long affordability efforts, I felt increasingly confirmed that I was approaching a career hinge moment. It was scary and unsettling—but also a bit freeing.

You see, I had been feeling restless in my job for quite some time. I now see how I was trying to add responsibilities and increase the complexity of what I was doing, perhaps as a way of keeping me engaged. Throughout life I have always been drawn to a challenge, and when I arrived at Gordon, some of the challenges seemed so daunting. It was, after all, my first time to lead an institution. But over time, my colleagues and I rose to meet each of them; eventually I got to the point where the challenges were no longer new, just different.

I began to assume more external duties and responsibilities, and I enjoyed them. Even so, I could see that I had built a team that was exceedingly qualified to lead the institution, but they needed a leader who was excited about Gordon's next season. I increasingly felt that was not me. Pondering these realities freed me in some helpful ways to begin thinking about future possibilities, but it also created space for me to grieve the process of leaving something behind or no longer being needed.

At the end of the summer, Rebecca and I spent several days on Nantucket in a beautiful setting where we could walk, pray, and consider options. We concluded that the signals for a change at work aligned with indications on the home front. Our twins would be finishing elementary school at the end of the academic year, and our oldest daughter would also be ready for a transition. If the Lindsays were to make a move, this year would be the ideal moment.

So almost precisely one year after the arrival of the first butterflies in my stomach, I announced my decision to step down as Gordon's president. By this point, I had passed through the discernment and anticipation phases of a transition, but without another job in hand, I spent more time than I wanted in the intersection phase of this particular hinge moment. The liminal state of being betwixt and between felt somewhat like a wilderness for me spiritually. I was confident that God had released me from Gordon, but I had no idea where he was calling us next. Even as I write these words, I am not sure what our next chapter will look like.

But I rest upon the assurance that I have known in my gut for many years and throughout every other hinge moment in my life—namely, that if we trust in the Lord with all of our heart, as it says in Proverbs 3, and lean not on our own understanding, if we acknowledge God in all of our ways, he will direct our paths.

# ACKNOWLEDGMENTS

Finishing a book project in the midst of a global pandemic underscored to me the importance of family, friends, and partners in bringing our hopes and dreams to reality. In addition to the hundreds of leaders who graciously agreed to be part of the PLATINUM Study (on which this book is based), I am deeply indebted to the amazing Gordon students and colleagues who helped me work on this manuscript and my ongoing responsibilities as this project came to completion. To my extraordinary Presidential Fellows—Henry, Dave, Sam, Ean, Kelley, Chase, Claire, Andrew, Dorothy, Antonio, Noah, Davis, Michael, Jordan, Josh, and Sarah-Catherine—thank you for doing whatever it took! I am also blessed with an amazing group of Cabinet colleagues at Gordon College, and their servant-leadership inspires me. Thank you Janet, Mark, Sandy, Britt, William, Larry, Chris, Stephen, Jewerl, Nick, Rick, and Dan. I thank God for an incredibly supportive Board of Trustees at Gordon, and I especially thank the Executive Committee—Herman, Mike, Mark, Gordon, Lisa, Dot, Sam, Peter, Bill, and Carrie—for their encouragement along the way.

A number of friends cheered me along during my time at Gordon, and their partnership and encouragement buoyed my spirits in very important ways. Thank you Denise and Steve Adams, Ellie and Dave Beatty, Mike Bontrager, Tim Breene, Colby

Burke, Todd Chapman, Barbara and Don Chase, Michael Cook, Catherine and Andy Crouch, Leslie and Bob Doll, Aimee and Chip Falcone, Tory and Bruce Farrell, Carolyn and Dan Fauber, Linda and Pat Gelsinger, John Goetz, Davi Gomes, Helen and Steve Hagen, Gayle and Gordon Hall, Price Harding, Peter Herschend, Shirley Hoogstra, Emily and Ross Jones, Elaine and John Kanas, Alice Lam and John Kong, Bonny and Caleb Loring, Mauro Meister, Renee and Mike Minogue, Joanna Mockler, Steve Moore, Solano Portela, Jose Inacio Ramos, Dante Rutstrom, Wai-Kwong Seck, Lyn and Tom Shields, Catherine and Chris Smith, Alice Tsang and Ken Mak, Sherry Tupper and Jackie Hipp, Ted Wieber, Meirwyn Walters, Brad and Pam Warner, Jenny and Woody White, Polly and Marv Wilson, and Guowei and Dan Wright. I also deeply appreciate all I have learned from my fellow directors at the Baylor Honors College, Christianity Today, Mercy Ships, and the Veritas Forum. And the K-12 Christian heads of school that have become partners and friends through the NEXT conference mean more than they likely realize. Finally, Debbi, Josh, and William have become not just an amazing team in the president's office at Gordon but great friends and partners in the Gospel. I will miss you very much!

This book touts the value of community as we navigate transitions in life, and Rebecca and I have benefited a great deal from several groups who have supported us throughout many hinge moments in our lives. We love and appreciate the presidential couples of the Broadmoor Collective and the Christian College Consortium and thank God for friends from Houston (especially the Bowers, Childers, Ecklund, Edwards, Gregory, Jenkins, Patterson, and Tour families) and from Boston (especially the Kims,

Nelsons, and Tucks). My fellow Eulogists have spoken grace and truth into my life over the last several years, and Gary Cook, Brad Eubank, John Rodgers, and Bill Townsend have done that same thing for decades.

I deeply appreciate Bob Fryling's friendship, who encouraged me years ago to consider InterVarsity Press as a publishing partner for this book and then introduced me to Jeff Crosby and Cindy Bunch, who stewarded this project at IVP so well. I have loved working with several staff members at IVP (especially Andrew Bronson and Elissa Schauer), and I am excited to see how God will use this book for his purposes. I am deeply grateful that this project reconnected me with Betsy Stokes, whose editorial talent is superb and whose contributions strengthened this book considerably. Of course, none of this would have been possible if Davis Metzger had not come to Gordon, led so well on our campus as student body president, and then worked in my office, eventually becoming a treasured conversation and writing partner in drafting this manuscript. Our future is very bright with emerging leaders like Davis assuming greater responsibility in the years ahead.

Finally, we encounter the most formative hinge moments of life in the context of our families, and I am forever grateful for the love and support of my mom as well as Dad and Janet, and the wonderful family I married into with Anne Elizabeth and Ronnie, Laura and Ron, and Margaret and Bill. And I am the most blessed man to be married to Rebecca, whose companionship along all of the hinge moments of my life has made all of the difference. It's a joy and privilege for us to provide similar support to Elizabeth, Caroline, and Emily as they navigate the hinge moments of their own lives and, Lord willing, as they help others do the same.

# QUESTIONS FOR DISCUSSION AND REFLECTION

## DAVIS METZGER

### 1 APPROACHING THE DOORS IN OUR LIVES: CONSIDERING A CHANGE

1. Looking back on your childhood, what was your "expected life story"—that vision for your future that you picked up from your family and your community about what your life should look like as an adult?

2. Describe a time when you were especially unprepared to handle a new situation. How did you manage the situation?

3. Describe a time when you grew restless while preparing for a change that emerged in your life.

4. What has been the biggest transition in your life so far?

## 2 STANDING OUTSIDE: WHY CHANGE HURTS YOUR HEAD

1. Describe recent examples in which you engaged System One and System Two thinking.

2. Has there been a time in your life in which you were more cautious than you should have been? What drove you to be particularly cautious?

3. What is one prediction you had for your life that has come true? What's one that has not come true so far?

4. What is an example of an unexpected fruit (good thing) that emerged in a new situation after you went through some kind of change?

## 3 STRADDLING THE THRESHOLD: THE SPACE BETWEEN SPACES

1. Who has been a significant mentor in your life? How did you meet?

2. Have you ever felt stuck in the space between spaces as you navigate a change in your life? Explain.

## 4 THE WELCOME MAT: LANDING IN YOUR NEW SPACE

1. Describe a time when someone (perhaps yourself) made a really bad first impression.

2. Describe a time when you had expectations for a new setting that were misplaced or wrong. How did God redeem that situation?

3. What is one contribution you have made to the culture of your family, your school, your church, or your place of work?

## 5 THE DEADBOLT: EARNING THE KEY THROUGH TRUST

1. Describe a time when you have had to be vulnerable even though it was difficult.

2. Have you ever seen someone in your workplace shade the truth or get caught in a lie that came back to hurt them? What were the results?

3. Describe a time someone demonstrated remarkable kindness to you when you were new to a situation.

4. When and in what kind of situation have you felt most needed?

## 6 THE HINGE: THE VIRTUE OF AFFIXED FLEXIBILITY

1. Name a time when being brave was difficult but rewarding for you.

2. What is one area of your life in which you have needed to cultivate greater self-control?

3. What does justice look like in your family, school, community, or line of work?

4. Describe two hinges on which your life hangs. What constant values are most important to you?

## 7 PASSAGES: GROWING THROUGH MAJOR LIFE CHANGES

1. When was a time that fear of loss kept you from making a change in your life?

2. Has God ever pushed you toward a calling or situation for which you felt unprepared? How did he equip you?

3. What has been your most formative failure so far?

4. What is the biggest lesson you have learned thus far after experiencing a major change in life?

## CONCLUSION

1. How might God be nudging you to embrace a change or transition in the near future?

2. What is one prayer you have for your future self that may come true through that possible change?

3. What do you expect to be your next hinge moment?

# NOTES

## INTRODUCTION

[1]Adam Chandler, "Why Do Americans Move So Much More Than Europeans?" *The Atlantic*, October 21, 2016, www.theatlantic.com/business/archive/2016/10/us-geographic-mobility/504968/.

[2]US Bureau of Labor Statistics, "Number of Jobs, Labor Market Experience, and Earnings Growth: Results from a National Longitudinal Survey Summary," August 22, 2019.

[3]Jeanne Meister, "The Future of Work: Job Hopping Is the 'New Normal' for Millennials," *Forbes*, August 14, 2012, www.forbes.com/sites/jeannemeister/2012/08/14/the-future-of-work-job-hopping-is-the-new-normal-for-millennials/#5ce9f33713b8.

[4]Demographic Intelligence, "COVID Family Survey," report of findings, June 2020.

[5]PLATINUM stands for "Public Leaders in America Today and the Inquiry into their Networks, Upbringing, and Motivations." As a precious metal, platinum also symbolizes the elite success of the participants of this study and the durability of their influence even through seasons of intense testing and pressure.

[6]Oprah Winfrey, "Who You Were Meant to Be—Everybody Has a Calling," Oprah's Lifeclass, video, October 17, 2011, www.oprah.com/oprahs-lifeclass/lesson-6-who-you-were-meant-to-be-everybody-has-a-calling_1.

## 1 APPROACHING THE DOORS IN OUR LIVES: CONSIDERING A CHANGE

[1]Report by the comptroller of the United States in "Improvements Being Made in Flood Fighting Capabilities in the Jackson Mississippi Area," United States Government Accountability Office, December 18, 1979, 1.

[2]Ann Swidler, "Culture in Action: Symbols and Strategies," *American Sociological Review* 51, no. 2 (1986): 273.

## 2 STANDING OUTSIDE: WHY CHANGE HURTS YOUR HEAD

[1]Daniel Kahneman, *Thinking, Fast and Slow* (New York: Farrar, Straus, and Giroux, 2011).

[2]Steven Levitt, "Heads or Tails: The Impact of a Coin Toss on Major Life Decisions and Subsequent Happiness," National Bureau of Economic Research, working paper 22487, August 2016, www.nber.org/papers/w22487.

[3]Brad Plumer, "Only 27 Percent of College Grads Have a Job Related to Their Major," *Washington Post*, May 20, 2013, www.washingtonpost.com/news/wonk/wp/2013/05/20/only-27-percent-of-college-grads-have-a-job-related-to-their-major/.

[4]The Beatles, *The Beatles Anthology* (San Francisco: Chronicle, 2000).

[5]William Burnett and David J. Evans, *Designing Your Life: How to Build a Well-Lived, Joyful Life* (New York: Knopf, 2016).

[6]Burnett and Evans, *Designing Your Life*, 67.

[7]Ewing Marion Kauffman Foundation, "Young Invincibles Policy Brief," November 10, 2011, www.kauffman.org/entrepreneurship/reports/young-invincibles-policy-brief-new-poll-finds-more-than-half-of-millenials-want-to-start-businesses-access-to-capital-and-lack-of-knowhow-are-key-barriers/.

[8]Denver Frederick with Dave Blanchard, interview on "The Business of Giving," May 31, 2017, https://denverfrederick.wordpress.com/2017/05/31/dave-blanchard-co-founder-and-president-of-praxis-labs-joins-denver-frederick/.

[9]Todd Sedmak, "Fall Enrollments Decline for 8th Consecutive Year," National Student Clearinghouse, December 16, 2019, www.studentclearinghouse.org/blog/fall-enrollments-decline-for-8th-consecutive-year/.

[10]Émile Durkheim, *Moral Education* (New York: Free Press, 1961), 148.

[11]John Gramlich, "Young Americans Are Less Trusting of Other People—and Key Institutions—Than Their Elders." Pew Research Center, August 6, 2019, www.pewresearch.org/fact-tank/2019/08/06/young-americans-are-less-trusting-of-other-people-and-key-institutions-than-their-elders/.

[12]Hugh Heclo, *On Thinking Institutionally* (New York: Oxford University Press, 2011), 110.

## 3 STRADDLING THE THRESHOLD: THE SPACE BETWEEN SPACES

[1]"Workplace Loyalties Change, but the Value of Mentoring Doesn't," *Knowledge@Wharton* (blog and podcast), May 16, 2007, https://knowledge.wharton.upenn.edu/article/workplace-loyalties-change-but-the-value-of-mentoring-doesnt/.

[2]Stefanie Baier et al., "Intent to Persist in College Freshmen: The Role of Self-Efficacy and Mentorship," *Journal of College Student Development* 57, no. 5 (2016): 614-19.

[3]See, for instance, Anat Prior, and Tamar H. Gollan, "Good Language-Switchers Are Good Task-Switchers: Evidence from Spanish-English and Mandarin-English Bilinguals," *Journal of the International Neuropsychological Society* 17, no. 4 (2011): 682-91. See also David W. Green and Jubin Abutalebi, "Language Control in Bilinguals: The Adaptive Control Hypothesis," *Journal of Cognitive Psychology* 25, no. 5 (2013): 515-30.

[4]Susan Bobb and Judith F. Kroll, "Words on the Brain: The Bilingual Mental Lexicon," in *Bilingual Cognition and Language: The State of the Science Across Its Subfields*, Studies in Bilingualism 54, ed. David Miller et al. (Amsterdam: John Benjamins, 2018).

## 4 THE WELCOME MAT: LANDING IN YOUR NEW SPACE

[1]Brian Holtz, "From First Impression to Fairness Perception: Investigating the Impact of Initial Trustworthiness Beliefs." *Personnel Psychology* 68, no. 3 (2014): 499-546.

[2]Dale Carnegie et al., *How to Win Friends and Influence People* (New York: Simon & Schuster, 1936).

[3]Frank Bernieri, "The Influence of Handshakes on First Impression Accuracy," *Journal of Social Influence* 6, no. 2 (April 2011): 78-87.

[4]"6 in 10 Employees Say Job Realities Different Than Expected; Glassdoor Survey," *Glassdoor* (blog), May 10, 2013, www.glassdoor.com/employers /blog/6-in-10-employees-say-job-realities-different-than-expected-glassdoor -survey/.

[5]NASA, "Mars Climate Orbiter Arrival Press Kit," September 1999, https://mars .nasa.gov/internal_resources/812/.

[6]NASA, "Mars Climate Orbiter Mishap Investigation Board Phase I Report," November 10, 1999.

[7]If you've never read it, it's worth looking up: William Shakespeare, *Henry V*, 4.3.18-67.

[8]Andy Crouch, *Playing God: Redeeming the Gift of Power* (Downers Grove, IL: InterVarsity Press, 2013); Albert Louis Zambone, "But What Do You Think, Ken Myers?" *Re:generation Quarterly* 6, no. 3 (2000).

[9]Max Weber and Guenther Roth, *Economy and Society: An Outline of Interpretive Sociology* (Berkeley: University of California Press, 1978).

## 5 THE DEADBOLT: EARNING THE KEY THROUGH TRUST

[1]Arthur Brooks and John Carr, "Religion, Economics, and New Approaches to Poverty," Faith Angle Forum, November 2015, https://faithangle.org/session /religion-economics-new-approaches-poverty/.

[2]Christian Smith, *Moral, Believing Animals: Human Personhood and Culture* (New York: Oxford University Press, 2009).

[3]Marshall Poe, *A History of Communications: Media and Society from the Evolution of Speech to the Internet* (New York: Cambridge University Press, 2011).

[4]S. V. Subramanian, Daniel Kim, and Ichiro Kawachi, "Social Trust and Self-Rated Health in U.S. Communities: A Multilevel Analysis," *Journal of Urban Health* 79, supp. 1 (2002): S21-34.

[5]Jon Jachimowicz et al., "Community Trust Reduces Myopic Decisions of Low-Income Individuals," *Proceedings of the National Academy of Sciences* 114, no. 21 (May 2017): 5401-6.

[6]Research cited in this section is from Paul Zak, "The Neuroscience of Trust," *Harvard Business Review*, January–February 2017, https://hbr.org/2017/01/the-neuroscience-of-trust.

[7]Stephen Covey, *The Speed of Trust: The One Thing That Changes Everything* (New York: Free Press, 2006).

[8]Angela Duckworth, Christopher Peterson, Michael Matthews, and Dennis Kelly, "Grit: Perseverance and Passion for Long-term Goals," *Journal of Personality and Social Psychology* 92, no. 6 (2007): 1087-1101.

[9]Thomas Lee and Angela Duckworth, "Organizational Grit," *Harvard Business Review*, September-October 2018, https://hbr.org/2018/09/organizational-grit.

[10]Lee and Duckworth, "Organizational Grit."

## 6 THE HINGE: THE VIRTUE OF AFFIXED FLEXIBILITY

[1]Marcus Aurelius, *Meditations: A New Translation*, trans. Gregory Hays (New York: Modern Library, 2002), 17.

[2]Marion Lloyd, "Soviets Close to Using A-Bomb in 1962 Crisis, Forum Is Told," *Boston Globe*, October 13, 2002, A20.

[3]Bradley Wright and David Carreon, "Can You Control Yourself?," *Christianity Today*, May 2017, 36.

[4]Wright and Carreon, "Can You Control Yourself?," 39.

[5]N. T. Wright, *After You Believe: Why Christian Character Matters* (New York: HarperCollins, 2010), 20-21.

[6]Aristotle, *The Nicomachean Ethics*, trans. Hugh Tredennick (New York: Penguin, 1976), 196.

[7]I am deeply indebted to the insights of Kenneth Bailey on the parable of the good Samaritan. See his *Jesus Through Middle Eastern Eyes: Cultural Studies in the Gospels* (Downers Grove, IL: IVP Academic, 2008).

## 7 PASSAGES: GROWING THROUGH MAJOR LIFE CHANGES

[1]Daniel Kahneman, and Amos Tversky, "Prospect Theory: An Analysis of Decision Under Risk," *Econometrica* 47, no. 2 (1979): 263-92.

[2]Edmund Burke, *Letters on a Regicide Peace* (Carmel, IN: Liberty Fund, 1999 [1796]).

[3]Ran Abramitzky et al. "To the New World and Back Again: Return Migrants in the Age of Mass Migration," *Industrial and Labor Relations Review* 72, no. 2 (2017): 300-322.

[4]Abramitzky et al. "To the New World and Back Again."

[5]Frederick Buechner, *Telling Secrets* (New York: Harper Collins, 1995).

[6]For more on this, see Eugene Peterson, *Under the Unpredictable Plant: An Exploration in Vocational Holiness* (Grand Rapids, MI: Eerdmans, 1994).

## CONCLUSION

[1]Posidippus, "Emblem 122" in *The Greek Anthology* 16.275, trans. W. R. Paton, Loeb Classical Library 86 (Cambridge, MA: Harvard University Press, 1918).